A Complete History

of Cornwall

A Complete History

of Cornwall

Thomas Cox

The Cornovia Press

SHEFFIELD

Published by The Cornovia Press in 2020

Originally published in 1720 by Thomas Cox as part of
Magna Britannia et Hibernia, Antiqua & Nova.

This edition © Chris Bond 2020

ISBN 978 1 908878 20 5

Contents

INTRODUCTION

Thomas Cox's *Magna Britannia et Hibernia, Antiqua et Nova*, to give it its abridged title, was compiled by 'an impartial hand' and sold in monthly parts which eventually comprised six quarto volumes, published between the years 1720 and 1731. The Reverend Thomas Cox was, according to R.M. Wiles[1], assisted by The Reverend Anthony Hall, who penned the Introduction as well as the county of Berkshire. Cox had originally advertised for contributions from all over the British Isles and the information gathered was, again according to Wiles[2], to be originally included as part of Herman Moll's *Atlas Geographus*, published as a monthly magazine between 1708 and 1717 as a text accompaniment to Moll's maps.

The sheer amount of information eventually accumulated by Cox outgrew its original purpose and necessitated a new publication. *Magna Britannia* was accompanied by the maps of Robert Morden, created at the beginning of the 18th century, and printed by Elizabeth Nutt, whose late husband had previously published Herman Moll's *Atlas Geographus*.

The Cornwall section was included as part of the first volume of *Magna Britannia*, originally published in its entirety in 1720, though some of the monthly partworks were listed in Lintott's *Monthly Catalogue* in 1714 and 1715[3], so it is uncertain when the *Compleat History of Cornwal* section first appeared.

---

1   Wiles, R.M., 1957 (2010 edition). *Serial Publication in England Before 1750*, Cambridge University Press, pp85-87.

2   *Ibid.*

3   *Ibid.*

My own copy is the 1720 edition, but the title page was damaged and has been replaced with the title page of the 1730 edition, a facsimile of which is included here.

The work builds on the earlier histories and topographies of Camden, Norden, Carew and Leland, but includes much contemporary information sent in by various correspondents. Many of the details of the boroughs have been based on those in Browne Willis's *Notitia Parliamentaria Or An History of the Counties Cities and Boroughs in England and Wales*, published in 1716, later than the listing in Lintot's *Monthly Catalogue*. It may therefore be inferred that in all likelihood the Cornwall section was primarily compiled, or at least completed, shortly before 1720. Of course Browne Willis may himself have used information originally compiled by Cox, though at present there is no evidence to suggest this.

Morden's map was originally produced in 1701[4] and is finely detailed, though small, being about 21 x 16cms and printed on a sheet roughly 30 x 21cms which fits snugly into *Magna Britannia's* quarto format when folded down the centre. Morden's previous map of Cornwall, that included with the 1695 edition of Camden's *Britannia*, is twice the size, but the 'Morden Miniatures', as they are commonly known, contain most of the information included in those earlier maps. Robert Morden was a prolific and highly respected mapmaker in the late 17th century and although he died in 1703 his maps were still regularly used throughout the rest of the 18th century. A full-size facsimile of the map is included shortly hereafter.

The printer of the six-volume set, Elizabeth Nutt, née Carr, was a very interesting character. Elizabeth was originally a 'Mercury Woman', selling newspapers and pamphlets on the streets of London, an activity which was likely to engender much familiarity with the Justices of the Peace. In 1692

---

4   Morden, Robert, 1701. *The New Description and State of England*, London.

Elizabeth Carr married John Nutt and later bought herself a retail business while her husband acquired a printing press. In 1705 John obtained a patent to print law books, which, alongside newspapers and pamphlets, were sold at the shop by The Royal Exchange. After his death in 1716 Elizabeth took over the printing business, with her son Richard managing the presses. He took over the law book patent in 1722. Her three daughters Sarah, Catherine and Alice were thereafter employed in the management of the several bookstores and newspaper stalls throughout London as the business expanded. Elizabeth continued in business until her death in 1746[5].

Cornwall in the 1720s was full of activity. Steam engines had recently been introduced and work was underway at Dolcoath to extract copper. Thomas Newcomen installed one of his atmospheric engines at Wheal Fortune in 1720 and the noted

5   Hunt, Margaret. 'Elizabeth Nutt' in Matthew, H.C.G. and Brian Harrison, eds, 2004. *The Oxford Dictionary of National Biography*, vol. 41, pp291-2. London: Oxford University Press.

playwright Samuel Foote was born in Truro that same year. Much of the landscape was about to radically change as the Industrial Revolution took hold. Cox's topographical account is therefore a valuable insight into a world about to change in ways unimaginable to many of its inhabitants.

The main body of the text is a topographical account of Cornwall, arranged in the form of a somewhat circuitous journey from Land's End to Saltash. Earls, Dukes, Baronets and other "worthies" are then given due note before we take in a brief Natural History concerning the geology, language, inhabitants, livestock, vegetation and produce and, naturally, with special attention given to mining and Stannary Laws.

An Ecclesiastical History then follows outlining the history of Christianity in Cornwall as well as giving details of some of the saints, the various religious institutions and of the charity schools. Then follows a detailed account of the boroughs of Cornwall, their voting rights and Members of Parliament, much of it replicating, as stated above, the account given in Browne Willis's *Notitia Parliamentaria*.

Finally is a reasonably comprehensive A-Z gazetteer of the towns, villages and parishes of Cornwall, complete with archaic spelling and with a few errors thrown in for good measure. I have omitted to include here the column devoted to Seats of the Gentry, partly due to size constraints and issues of legibility, though in my defence only one seat is given in the entire original gazetteer, that being Crew-Hall in Borrow[6]. Despite my modest expertise in such matters I am none the wiser as to where this refers to, so its omission is therefore considered to be a minor inconvenience.

---

6   There is a Crew Hall, or Crewe Hall, in Cheshire. It appears in the top row of the second page of the gazetteer for Cheshire, the exact same place as it appears in the Cornwall gazetteer, and so it is likely that its appearance in Cornwall is an error. Borrow in Stratton could refer to either Borough in Whitstone or Borough in Bridgerule.

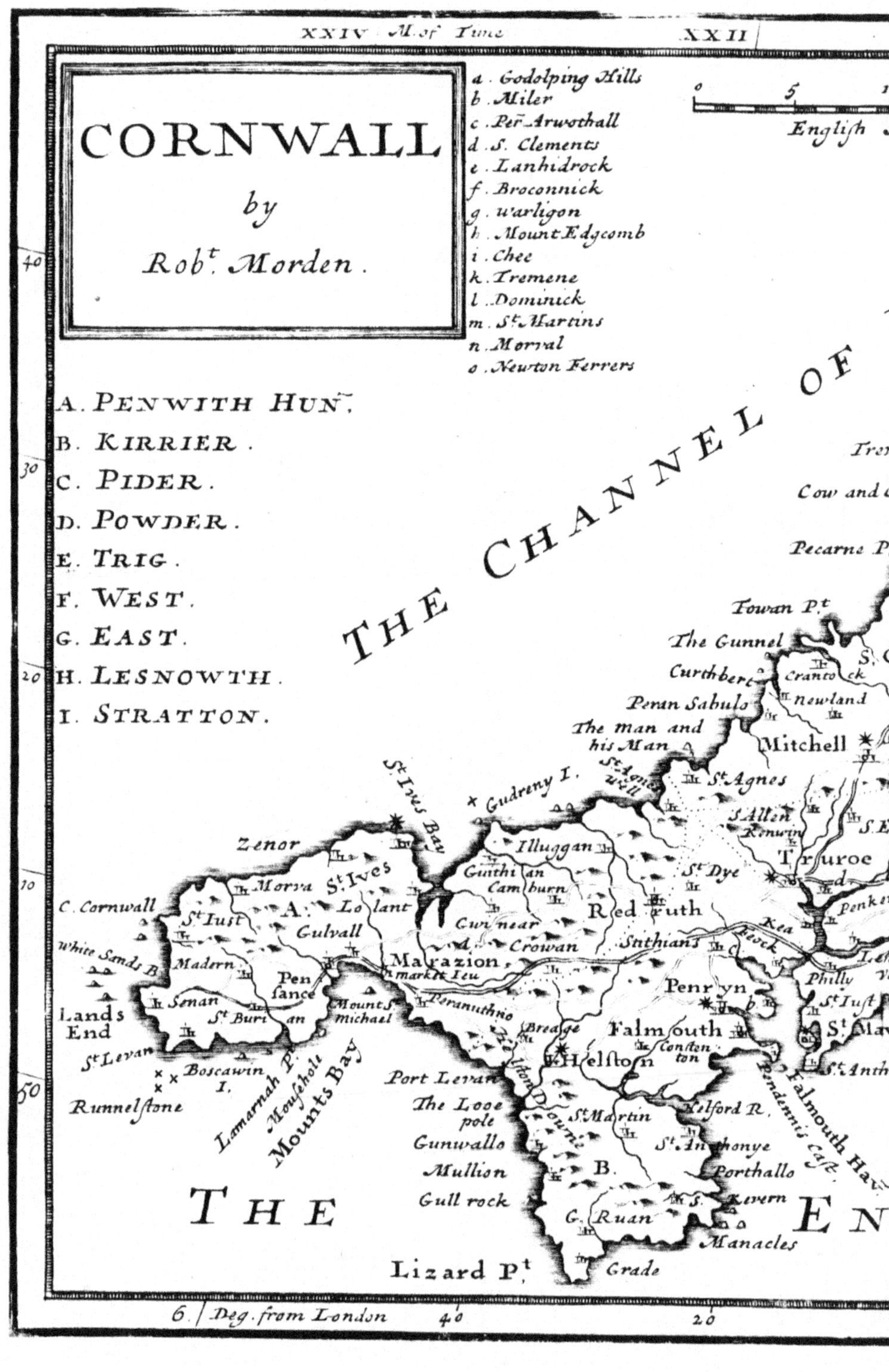

XXIV M. of Time XXII
a. Godolping Hills
b. Miler
c. Peñ Arwothall
d. S. Clements
e. Lanhidrock
f. Broconnick
g. Warligon
h. Mount Edgcomb
i. Chee
k. Tremene
l. Dominick
m. St. Martins
n. Morval
o. Newton Ferrers
0   5   10
English M.
CORNWALL
by
Robt. Morden.
A. PENWITH HUNᵗ.
B. KIRRIER.
C. PIDER.
D. POWDER.
E. TRIG.
F. WEST.
G. EAST.
H. LESNOWTH.
I. STRATTON.
THE CHANNEL OF
Trevo
Cow and Ca
Pecarne Pᵗ
Towan Pᵗ
The Gunnel
Curthberi
Cranto ck
S. C
Peran Sabulo
newland
The man and
his Man
Mitchell
Gudreny I.
St. Agnes well
St. Agnes
S. Allen
Renwin
S. Ea
Zenor
Illuggan
Truroe
Morva St. Ives
St. Ives Bay
Ginthi an
Camburn
St. Dye
d
C. Cornwall
Lolant
Red ruth
Penkevi
St. Iust
Gulvall
Gwinear
Kea
Le
White Sands B.
Madern
Crowan
Stithians
Rock
Philly
Ver
Marazion
Lands
market Ieu
Penryn
St. Iust
End
Pen
sance
Peranuthno
Senan
St. Burian
Mounts
Michael
Breage
Falmouth
St. Maw
St. Levan
Conston
ton
St. Anthon
Boscawin
I.
Lamarnah Pᵗ
Mouseholl
H. Helston
Runnelstone
Mounts Bay
Port Levan
The Looe
pole
St. Martin
Kelford R.
Porthallo
Gunwallo
St. Anthonye
Mullion
B.
Gull rock
G. Ruan
Kevern
THE
Manacles
Lizard Pᵗ
Grade
EN
6. Deg. from London   40   20

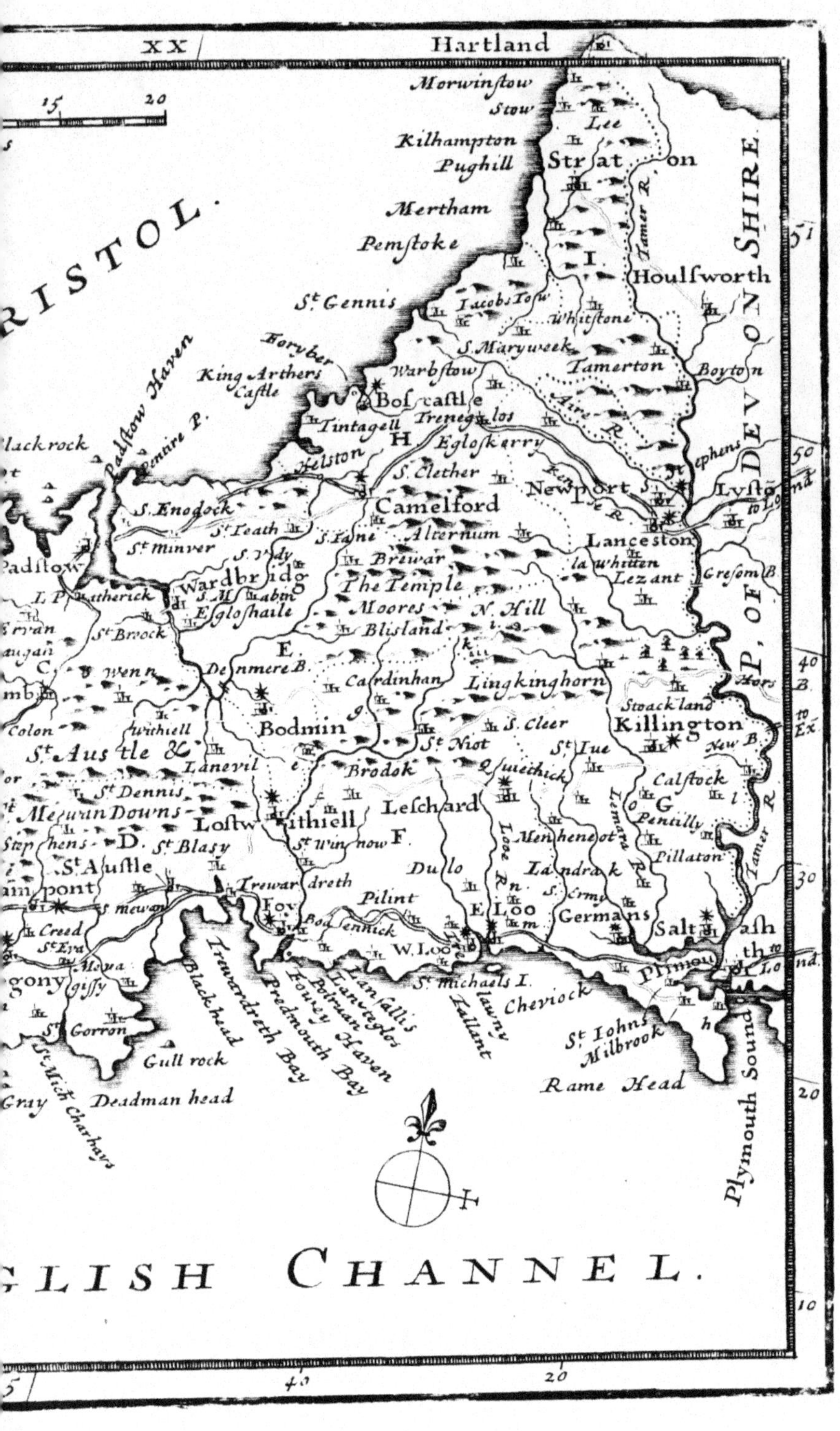

XX
Hartland
15 20
Morwinstow
Stow
Lee
Kilhampton
Pughill
Strat on
Mertham
Pemstoke
I.
St Gennis
Jacobs Tow
Houlsworth
Whitstone
Foryber
Warbstow
Tamerton
Boyton
King Arthers Castle
Boscastle
Padstow Haven
Tintagell
Treneglos
Aire R.
Helston
H
Egloskerry
Kent R.
Stephens
DEVONSHIRE
Blackrock
S. Clether
Newport
Lyston
S. Enodock
Camelford
Lanceston
St Teath
St Tane
Alternum
la whitten
St minver
S. Udy
Brewar
Lezant
Gresom B.
Padstow
Wardbridg
The Temple
L. P. atherick
Eglosshaile
Moores
N. Hill
St Brock
Blisland
Wenn
Denmere B.
Cardinhan
Lingkinghorn
Stoackland
Killington
Colon
withiell
Bodmin
S. Cleer
St Iue
New B.
St Austle
Lanevil
St Niot
Calstock
G
St Dennis
Brodok
Quiechick
Pentilly
Mewan Downs
Lostwithiell
Leschard
Menhennot
Pillaton
Stephens
D
St Blasy
St Winnow
F
St Austle
Dullo
Landrak
Trewardreth
Pilint
E Loo
Germans
Saltash
Fov
Bodennick
W. Loo
St Michaels I.
Cheviock
Plymouth
Creed
St Era
St Johns
Meva
Milbrook
gony
gissy
Trewardreth Bay
Fowey Haven
Predmouth Bay
Lanteglos
Lansallis
Polruan
Tawny Tallant
St Gorron
Gull rock
Rame Head
Gray
Deadman head
ENGLISH CHANNEL.

A COMPLEAT

HISTORY

OF

CORNWAL.

CONTAINING,

1. The *Geographical Defcription* of the County in Alphabetical Order. 2. The *Ecclefiaftical Hiftory.* 3. The *Civil Hiftory.* 4. The *Natural Hiftory.* 5. The *Literary Hiftory.* 6. The *Antiquities.* 7. A *Map* of the County. 8. A *Table* of the Names of all the *Towns* and *Villages, &c.* with the Value of the Livings, the Patrons, Incumbents, and Gentlemens Seats : Alfo a Scheme of all the Market-Towns, *&c.* their Diftance from *London,* and from one another, *&c.*

In the *SAVOY.*

Printed by E. and R. Nutt; and Sold by T. Cox, at the *Lamb* under the *Royal Exchange, Cornhill.* M.DCC.XXX.
[Price 1 s. 6 d.]

Cornwal.

THIS County and *Devonshire* was the Country inhabited by those *Britains* which *Solinus* calls *Dunmonii*, and *Ptolomy Danmonii*, from *Dun* an Hill, and *Moina* a Mine, because these Parts have been always famous for Hills of Tin Mines. Mr. *Camden* is of Opinion, that the *Ostidamnii*, called also *Ostæi* and *Ostiones*, were the same with these *Dunmonii*, because *Strabo* says, they were seated on the Western Ocean, in the remotest Parts of *Europe*, over against *Spain*, not far from the island *Uxantissa*, or *Ushant* ; which Circumstances exactly agree to the Country of the *Danmonii*. This County reached out to the Westward the farthest of all *Britain* ; and being inhabited by the Remains of the Western *Britains*, who fled hither for Shelter against the *Saxons*, it took the Name of *Cornwal*, partly from the Figure of the Land, which runs out into Promontories like Horns, called by the *Britains*, *Kernaw*, and partly from these later Inhabitants, whom the *Saxons* called *Gauls* or *Waules*, which is the same as **Wealʃh**. And hence it is that *Cornwal* is called by some Writers *West Wales*.

The *Romans* were a great while in this Island, before

they reduced this Part of it ; and 'tis dubious whether they ever conquer'd it so absolutely, but the *British* Princes had the Dominion of it, either as Tributary or Independent ; for we find one *Dionotus* King of *Cornwall,* when *Maximus* usurp'd in *Britain.* After the *Saxon* Invasion, the *British* Dukes of *Cornwal* not only maintained their own Ground, but assisted the *Welsh* to keep their Country. For *Blederic* Duke of *Cornwal* joining with the King of *Wales,* defeated King *Ethelfrid* in a Battle near *Bangor,* and drove him beyond the *Humber.* These *Dukes* never submitted to the *Saxons* during the Heptarchy ; and tho' they assisted the *Danish* Invaders, who began about *A.D.* 835 to infest this Isle, against King *Egbert,* the victorious *Saxon* Monarch, and by him were conquer'd, yet they were still govern'd by their own Princes, who also had *Devonshire* subject to them. At last King *Athelstan* drove them out of *Devonshire,* and by Force of Arms obliged them to keep within the River *Tamar* : But whether he set a Governor over them, made them tributary to him, or contented himself with a bare Homage, History does not determine. [a] 'Tis certain, that *William* the Conqueror either annexed it to the rest of *England,* or found it so, because [b] he made *Robert de Morton* Earl of *Cornwal,* as we shall hereafter shew.

This County is bounded on the North, South, and West Sides, by the Sea, and is parted on the East from

---

a *We nd in our Writers several termed sometimes Kings, at other Times Dukes and Earls of* Cornwal, *as* Corineus, Madan, Leris, Cloterius, *Kings* ; Belinus, Tennancias, Asclepiodorus, Conan, Meridocke, Dionotus, Moigne, Caradoc, Cador, Blederic, Ivor, Dungarth, Alpsius, Orgerius, *and* Condor, *Dukes. But whether they held it as a Dignity or an Office under the* British *and* Saxon *Kings, 'tis impossible to find out, and therefore we have only given the Catalogue of them.*

b Condor, *the last* Saxon *Duke, immediately upon his Entrance on the Kingdom, did him Homage for his Dukedom, which he held but a little while before.*

Devonshire by the River *Tamar*, except a small Tract of Land, and so makes a *Peninsula*. The *British* Sea washes the South Coasts, the *Severn* Sea the North, and *St. George's* Chanel the West. The Length of it from E. to W. is about 70 Miles, and the Breadth upon the Borders of *Devon*, which is the widest Place, 40 ; but above *Gulval* and *St. Ives*, where 'tis narrowest, not above five. At the West End it shoots out into two Promontories, one called of old by the *Romans, Bolerium, Belerium,* or *Antivestæum* ; and by the *British* Historians, *Penwith* ; but by the Inhabitants in their own Language, *Pen von las, i.e.* The Ends of Earth ; and by us, the *Land's-End* : The other was named *Ocrinum* or *Danmoricum*, but is by the *English* named the *Lizard Point*. In the whole Space of Ground it contains nine Hundreds, 161 Parishes, 27 Market-Towns, of which 21 send [a] Members to Parliament ; six Castles, nine Parks, and 96000 Acres of Land.

The principal Rivers are, the *Tamar*, which runs into the Sea near *Plimouth* ; the *Camel*, which falls into the Chanel at *Padstow* Haven ; the *Fale*, which empties it self into the Sea at *Falmouth*, as the *Cober* does at *Helston*, and *Loo* at *Loo*. The *Liver* also and other Rivulets mingle with them in their Passage. Over them all are 32 Bridges.

We shall begin our Survey of this County with the utmost Promontory Westward, which 'tis very probable did extend it self much farther than now it does, but has long since been washed away by the Violence of the Sea, as is proved by the Pieces of Windows, Trees, and other Things, which have been taken up or discovered by Mar-

---

a   *In the ancient Parliament-Rolls, we find that* Ledeford *sent Members twice,* viz. *Anno* 28, & 30 *Edw.* I. *but never since.*

iners upon these Coasts.

The first Place of any Note is called *St. Buriens*, in *Penwith* Hundred, called anciently *Eglis Buriens, i.e.* The Church of *Beriana*, or *Buriana*, because it was dedicated to a certain religious *Irish* Woman of that Name ; for this Country hath all along paid so great Veneration to the *Irish* Saints, as well as to their own, that there is hardly a Town in the County but what is dedicated to some *Irish* or *Cornish* Saint. 'Tis said, that King *Athelstan* returning from his Conquest of the Islands of *Scilly*, built a Church here, and gave it the Privelege of a Sanctuary : But however that be, 'tis certain that in the Days of *William* the Conqueror here was a College of Prebendaries, to whom the neighbouring Grounds belonged. 'Tis at present an independent Deanery, formerly belonging to the Pope, but was seized into the King's Hands by one of the *Edwards*. It contains within its Jurisdiction the Parishes of *St. Burien, Sennan*, and *St. Leven* ; and the Bishops of *Exeter* holding it *in Commendam*, all Spritual Jurisdiction is so entirely lodged in them, that there lies no Appeal from them but to the King directly. In the Church here there is a remarkable Tomb in this Form :

The Border round it has a long Inscription but in such

antique Letters, as our best Antiquaries cannot read
them. From the Words, DA BOLLAIT, *i.e.* Of *Bolleit*,
they conjecture that the Name of the Person who lies buried under it goes before, because there is an House of that
Name in the Parish. At the Bottom of it are these Figures
M4p. 16. MCI. which may be supposed to mean, *March*
16. 1101. The whole Inscription may be seen in the Additions to *Camden* by Dr. *Gibson*.

In the Parish of *Sennan* above mentioned stands
Penros, not a Town, as Mr. *Camden* in his Map of the
County makes it, but only an House, which is at present
the Seat of *Henry James* Esq; whose Family has had it a
long time for their Mansion. Colonel *Jones,* who so emin-
ently distinguished himself in our late Wars with *Spain,*
and is now Governor of *Tortosa* in *Spain* under the Cath-
olick King, is of this Family.

Not far from this place is the Land called *Biscaro-*
woune, where are nineteen large Stones set in a Circle,
above 12 Foot distant one from another, and in the midst
stands one much larger and higher than any of the rest.
Mr. *Camden* conjectures them to have been some Trophy
of the *Romans* under their later Emperors, or of King
Athelstan the *Saxon* when he subdued *Cornwal* ; but other
learned Men more probably suppose them to be some
ancient Sepulchral Monument of the *Britains,* especially
since it plainly appears from certain Inscriptions on other
Stones, so set up on end, that they were such. Mr.
Edward Lhwyd, the *Welch* Antiquary, gives us an
Instance of one in *Wales,* encompassed with a Ditch
instead of Stones, thus inscribed, Mayest thou awake.
This Place is render'd farther worthy of Regard for giving Name to that ancient and worthy Family of the

Boscawens, of which *Hugh Boscawen* Esq; is, who has been a Member of Parliament for the County and several Corporations of it. Going from hence to the South, we come to

Mounts-Bay, where the Shore drawing in, makes a Bay in the Form of a New Moon. 'Tis called *Mounts-Bay*, because of a Rock, which they call *St. Michael's Mount*, standing in it. 'Tis a Tradition among the People here, that the Ocean breaking in violently, drowned that Part of the Country, which now is the Bay. This Bay is a very safe Harbour against the South Winds. Upon it lies *Mouse-hole*, called in the *British* Tongue Port *Inis*, or the Port of the Island, because there is a little Island lying before it. *Henry de Tiels*, a Baron, Lord of *Alwerton* and *Tiwernell*, procured the Privilege of a Market for this Place. Near which stands

Pensance, *i.e.* (as Mr. *Camden* interprets it) the Head of the Sand ; but the true Construction is the Head of the Saint, as may appear from the Arms of the Town, which are *John Baptist*'s Head in a Charger ; and if this did not put it beyond dispute, we might rather imagine the Original Name to be *Pensavas*, *i.e.* The Head of the Chanel, which would agree well to the Nature of the Place. It is but a little Market-Town, kept on *Thursdays*, but is very famous for, 1. Being near the noted Stone called *Main-Amber*, *i.e.* The Stone of *Ambrosius*, which tho' it was of a vast Bigness, a Man might make it move with one Finger in its proper Place, which a great number of Men could not remove it from. It was a great Rock, raised upon some others of a lesser Size, and so equally poized, that a little Force would shake it, tho' hardly any could displace it. It was thrown down in *Oliver's* Time by one *Shrubsall,* then Governor of *Pendennis* Castle, by undermining it with a great deal of Labour. 2. For *Maddren's* Well, by drinking of whose Water many great Cures have been effected, *viz.* A Cripple who had been forced to crawl on his Hands and Feet 16 Years ; two Men who had used many Prescriptions of Physicians and Surgeons without Benefit ; and a Rector of a neighbouring Parish, going to reprove some of his Parishioners for their superstitious use of it, and drinking of it. [a] Upon the same Bay stands

Merkju, another little Market-Town, which takes its Name from the Market, on *Thursdays,* it being a contraction of *Market Jupiter, i.e.* as 'tis now called *Market Jew,* or rather *Ju.* It is an ill Harbour.

St. Michael's Mount stands in the Corner of it. [b] 'Twas formerly called *Dinsol,* and by the *Cornish, Careg-cowse, i.e.* an Hoary Rock, and by the *Saxons,* Mychel-ſtop, *i.e. Michael's-Place.* 'Tis a Rock indifferent high and craggy, compassed with Water when the Tide is in, and joined to the main Land when 'tis out, and so the People say, 'Tis Land and Island twice a Day. *John* Earl of *Oxford,* [c] trusting to the Strength of the Place, fortified himself here against King *Edward*

---

a   *This Town, and Church of St.* Paul *in it, with* Mouse-hole *and* Newlin, *was burnt by the* Spaniards *in 1595, who with four Galleys surpriz'd the Country, and set the Farms and Villages on Fire. Sir* Francis Godolphin *did what he could to rally the affrighted People for their own and the Country's defence, but could do nothing till Help came from* Plimouth, *at his Request, and drove them home. This disaster the* Cornish *say was long before foretold in these verses ; —* Ewra teyre, &c. i.e. *There shall be Land upon the Rock of* Merlin : *Men that will burn* Paul's *Church,* Pensance, *and* Newlin ; *but being again rebuilt, is now a considerable Trading Town.*

b   *It was burnt by the* French *in the beginning of King* Henry VIII's *Reign, who came thither with 30 Sail of Ships.*

c   *After King* Henry VI. *was routed in* Barnet-*Field, whose Part he had taken.*

IV. and bravely defended it awhile ; but his Men at the first Assault yielded. Upon the Top of the Rock, within the Fort, [a] was a Chapel dedicated to *Michael* the Arch-Angel, and *William* Earl of *Cornwal* and *Moriton* built a Cell there for a Monk or two, who pretended that *St. Michael* had appeared to them there ; which credulous People believing, gave it the Name of *St. Michael's Mount.* [b] At the Bottom of this Mount, within the Memory of our Fathers, as they were digging for Tin, they found Spear-Heads, Battel-Axes, and Swords of Copper, all wrapt up in Linen, of the same Sort as those discover'd long ago in *Hircinia,* and lately in *Wales.* In the Rocks all along this Coast, the *Cornish* Chough, called *Pyrrhocorax,* from its red Bill and Feet, breeds. This Bird, as the Inhabitants know by sad Experience, is not only a Thief, and will steal Pieces of Money and hide them, but an Incendiary, and will privately set Houses on Fire. In this Place the Country is narrowest, being contracted into a sort of Isthmus, scarce four Miles cross to the *Severn* Sea. A little beyond the Mount is the Bay called

Mount's-Bay, from the Mount. 'Tis a very safe Harbour for Ships against the South and South-East Winds, being six or seven Fathom deep at low Water. More to the East lies

Godolphin, or (as it was anciently written) *Godolcan,* an Hill famous for store of Tin-Mines, but principally for that noble Family, who even in the Conqueror's Time were

---

a *King* Charles I. *imprison'd Duke* Hamilton *here, till the Parliament took it, and released him.*

b *It was made an* Asylum *by the* Cornish *Gentry and their Families in the last Rebellion there, and by the Lady* Ann Gordon, *Wife of* Perkin Warbeck *; but it secur'd neither.*

Lords of it, and took their Names from it. The first that we have upon Record is *David Godolphin*, Lord *Godolphin*, who leaving only one Daughter and Heir, called *Eleanor*, she was married to *John Rinsey*, of *Rinsey*, Esq; on Condition that he should assume the Name of *Godolphin*, and from her descended

Thomas Godolphin Esq; who was the father of

Sir *William Godolphin* Kt. and *John Godolphin* Esq; the Progenitor of the *Godolphins* of *Mosswall* and *Trewardoneth*.

Sir *William Godolphin* Kt. was the Father of

Sir *William Godolphin* Kt. (who died without Issue) and *Thomas*, the Father of

Sir [a] *Francis Godolphin*, who has Issue

Sir *William Godolphin* Kt. who had three Sons

Sir *Francis Godolphin* Kt. of the *Bath, Sidney* and *William*.

Sir *Francis Godolphin* has Issue four Sons,

Sir *William Godolphin*, created Baronet by King *Charles* II. in 1663, *Sidney, Henry*, and *Charles*.

Sidney, the second Son, was a Person of most excellent Accomplishments ; and being Burgess for *Helston* in *Cornwal* in several Parliaments, gave such Proofs of his Abilities, that he was employed in Embassies, managing the Treasury, and other Offices, in the Reigns of K. *Charles* and K. *James* II. and K. *William* III. and at

---

a   *This Gentleman was so great a Dealer in Tin, that he set 300 Men at work daily, and paid* 1000l. *a Year Customs to Qu.* Elizabeth, *and by his Labours and Inventions in the Tin Matters advanced the Benefit of the Trade so much, that the Customs were increased above* 10000l. *a Year to that Queen.*

length was made Lord High Treasurer by Qu. *Anne*, *A.D.* 1702, and Knight Companion of the noble Order of the Garter in 1704. In these Employments he was created by King *Charles* II. Baron *Godolphin* of *Rialton*, and after by Qu. *Anne* Viscount *Rialton* and Earl of *Godolphin, December* 29, 1706. He left only one Son,

Francis, now Earl of *Godolphin*, who married the Lady *Henrietta Churchill*, eldest Daughter and one of the Coheirs of *John* Duke of *Marlborough*, having Issue by her one Son and one Daughter, *William* Lord Viscount *Rialton*, and Lady *Henrietta*.

Henry Godolphin, the third Son of Sir *Francis*, is now Dean of St. *Paul's*, and Provost of *Eaton*.

Charles, the youngest, was a Commissioner of the Customs for many Years, and Auditor of *Wales*.

Their Name is said to signify a white Eagle, and therefore 'tis thought that this Family bears for their Arms, in a Shield *Gules*, an Eagle display'd between three *Fleurs-de-Lys Argent*.

From *Michael's-Mount* Southward there jets a Chersonese, at the Entrance of which we meet with

Helston, or (as the Inhabitants call it) *Hellas*, from the salt Water about it. 'Tis a Market and Borough Town, standing on the River *Cober*, and has the Privilege of stamping Tin, which they call Coinage, and sending two Members to Parliament. The Market is on *Saturdays*, and Fair *March* 13. A little lower, the Sea forms a great Lake of salt Water, called

Loopool, two Miles in Length, which might make a

convenient Haven, but that it is separated from the Sea by a Bank of Sand, which hinders the Entrance of Ships. Sometimes the Sea, by the Violence of the Waves and Wind, will break thro' the Bank, which, when it happens, it fills the Neighbourhood with an affrighting Noise. [a] At a little Distance from hence there is a Military Camp, which is called

Erth, built in a large Circumference, with great Stones heaped one upon another without Mortar, of which Sort some others are found up and down the Country, supposed to be made in the *Danish* Wars, and not unlike those *British* Fortifications which *Tacitus* thus describes, A rude and confus'd Structure of great Stones. Going along the Sea-Coasts, we come to the Peninsula called

Meneg, where the last mentioned Monument, called *Erth*, is contained. Mr. *Samms* (*Brit. p.*59) will have both these Names of *Phœnician* Original, to favour his Hypothesis, that this Part of *England* was peopled by the *Phœnicians*, who traded hither ; but these are uncertain Conjectures, not to be depended on. The whole Peninsula is well stocked with little Villages, and pretty large. 'Tis thought to be the same with that [b] *Menna* which *Jornandes* the *Goth* in his Geticks thus describes : It is the farthest Part of *Britain*, abounding with several Sorts of Metal, affording good Pasture, and in general contributing more to the nourishing of Cattle than Men ; which, if it were ever true, as to the Plenty of Metals, is now not so, for it is quite drained. The Mariners call it the *Lizard Point* ; and *Ptolomy*, *Damnonium* and *Ocrinum*, from *Ocra*, a craggy Mountain, perhaps, or rather from the

---

a   *This Pool breeds a kind of Bastard Trout, much exceeding such as live in the fresh Water in Bigness and Goodness.*

b   *Some Copies read* Memno.

British Word *Ochr*, an Edge, because this Promontory is pointed or edged like a Cone.

At the Entrance into this Peninsula, we meet with a Town called *Constanton*, where, about 30 Years since, near the Church, in a Place where once stood a Cross, (as is said) was found a Buff Bag full of Silver Pieces, some of King *Arthur*'s Coin, and some of King *Canute*'s, of which this is the Figure, the Reverse is not so perfect as to be read.

Eastward of *Meneg*, the Shore draws in again, and makes a Bay full of winding Creeks, into which the little River *Fale* discharges it self. In old Time a Town, which the Ancients called *Voluba*, stood on this River ; but that being destroyed long since, another is risen in its room at a little distance, which retains something of the old Name, and is called

Falmouth, or *Volemouth*, which is a spacious and excellent Haven, altogether as noble as *Brundusium* in *Italy*, and rival'd by *Plimouth* only, made by the falling of the River *Fale* into it. It is so large, that 100 Ships may ride in its winding Bays, at such a Distance that from no one of them shall be seen the Top of the others Main-mast. The Creeks, which rise on all Sides, are a sure Defence for the Ships against all Storms and Winds, which makes it much frequented. At the Entrance into the

Haven there is an high uneven Rock, called by the Inhabitants *Crage, i.e.* The Rock ; and each Side of it is fortified with a Castle, built by King *Henry* VIII. for the Safety of the Place, and Terror of his Enemies : That on the East Side is called *St. Maudits,* and that on the West *Pendinas,* or in common Speech *Pendennis,* of which an ancient Poet thus sings ;

Pendinas tenet, &c.

High on a craggy Rock Pendennis *stands,*

And with its thund'ring Guns the Port commands,

While strong St. Maudits *answers it below,*

Where Falmouth's *Sands the spacious Harbour show.*

King *William* III. of blessed Memory, settled here a Packet-Boat for a Communication with *Spain,* while we had an Alliance with that King, *Charles* II. but since his Death, and by reason of the War we had with *Spain* since, the Packet now goes to *Lisbon,* the chief City of *Portugal.*

The Castle of *Pendennis* is one of the largest in the Kingdom, and has usually a small Garrison in it. It held out for the King in the Civil Wars, till General *Fairfax* had almost put an end to them, and then it was taken by Colonel *Richard Fortescue* for the Parliament. The present Governor is Brigadier *Richard Munden,* the Son of Sir *Richard Munden* Kt. who took the Island of *St. Helena* from the *Dutch.* At *Falmouth* the King has also divers Officers, as a Collector, Customer and Comptroller for the Management of the Customs there. 'Tis a Corporation Town, and govern'd by a Mayor and Alder-men, but sends no Members to Parliament. The Market is on *Thursdays*, but chiefly for Corn and Meat, and Fair It has the Honour of giving the Title of Viscount to *George Fitz Roy*, third natural Son of K. *Charles* II. by the Dutchess of *Cleveland*, whom his Father, in the Year 1675, *October* 1, created Baron of *Pontefract*, Viscount *Falmouth*, and Earl of *Northumberland* ; which last Title he afterwards, in 1682, improved to the Title and Dignity of a Duke.

St. Maws or *St. Maudit*, the other Castle, has a little Town adjoining, which has the Honour of having its Rep-resentatives in Parliament. The Governor of it is, or lately was, *Hugh Boscawen* Esq; above mentioned. *Ptolomy* calls the Haven *Cenionis Ostium*, from the *British* Word *Geneu*, signifying a Mouth or Entrance, which *Tregenie*, a Town at the Mouth of the Harbour, confirms, because the name signifies a little Town, or if the *Phœnician* Derivation may pass, a Castle or Fort at the Mouth. 'Tis a Market and Borough Town, and sends its Representatives to Parliament. The Market is on   and the Fair on St. *Leonard's* Day. Above this Place, on the same River, stands

Grampound, another small Market and Borough Town. *John* of *Eltham*, Earl of *Cornwal*, younger brother of King *Edward* III. granted to the Burghers of this Place the whole Vale of *Grampound*, and all the Lands of *Coytfala*, which is in the *British* Tongue *Fala-wood*. The Charter of this Grant is still extant, and at this Day there are some Lands near the Town, and within the Precincts of the Borough, called *Coytfala*. Some think that this Town is the *Voluba* of the Ancients, because it stands upon same River *Vale*, and upon the building of the Bridge it was changed into *Ponsmur*, which in French is *Granpont*, or (as we now call it) *Grampound*. This is also a Market and Borough Town, sending Representatives to Parliament. Its Market is on *Saturdays*, and Fair   On the same Side of the River, by the Sea-Side lies

Tregonan, the Seat of the *Tredenhams*. Passing from *Grampound* to *Truro*, on the other Side of the *Fale*, you meet with a little Village called

Golden, the Seat and Manor of the *Tregians*, who have been a long time Owners of it, and matched to the best Families in the Shire. A little below, just at the Haven's Mouth, we find

Fenton-Gallon, *i.e. Hartswell*, which was lately the Seat of the ancient Family of [a] *Carminow*, who were of high Esteem in these Parts for Blood and Wealth. One of them, in the Reign of King *Edward* III. commenced a Suit in the Court of Chivalry with the Lord *Scroop* for his bearing in his Arms, in a Shield *Azure* a Bend *Or* : But the Matter was taken up, and referred to some of the most eminent Persons in the Kingdom. *John* of *Gaunt*, the famous Duke of *Lancaster*, upon whose Family, after many bloody Battels, the Crown was settled, was the Chief, and before him *Carminow* proved his Right, by the constant bearing of those Arms in his Family before the Conquest : But because his Opponent was a Baron of the Realm, it was agreed and determined, that the Lord *Scroop* should still bear the same Arms, but with a File in

---

a   *One of this Family served in Parliament for the County* 30 *K.* Edward I.

Chief for Distinction. This *Carminow* had this *Cornish* Motto to his Coat, *Catarag Whethow, i.e.* A Straw for a Dissembler. One Mr. *Carminow* liv'd here in the last Century, but his Family is now extinct, and the Estate is descended to the *Holcombs.* From hence we come to

Truro, on the West Side of the *Fale* so called from its three Streets, as the Word *Truru* in *Cornish* signifies. 'Tis almost encompassed with two little Rivers. Here also the Tin dug in these Parts is stamped. It has two Markets every Week, *viz.* on *Wednesdays* and *Saturdays,* four Fairs, and sends its Representatives to Parliament. It is accounted the chief Town in the Shire, where the Justices keep their Sessions for this Division. It is govern'd by a Mayor, Recorder, and 24 Capital Burgesses, of whom four are chosen Aldermen, and out of them the Mayor. The Church is a good old Structure, and in it are several Monuments of the *Roberts, Arundels, Michels,* and others. The chief Inn was once a Mansion-House of one of those Families, and round the Hall, according to the Custom of those Times, are their Arms engraved. 'Tis a Town of good Trade, because Vessels of considerable Burthen come up to it to load and unload. The famous Sir *John Arundel,* who took *Duncan Campbell,* the *Scotch* Pyrate, was born here. This Town is honour'd by giving the Title of Baron to *Richard Roberts,* of *Truro,* Esq; who for his signal Loyalty, as well as great Wealth, was by King *James* I. created a Baronet, *A.D.* 1616, and afterwards advanced to the Dignity of a Baron of this Realm, by the Title of Lord *Roberts* of *Truro.* How this Family have been since raised to the Earldom of *Radnor,* shall be spoken of in its proper Place. From *Truro,* following the Haven, we come, on the West Side, to

St. Michel, a Town of special Consideration in the *Saxon* Times, but now become a mean Borough, of not above 30 Houses, yet still retains the Privilege of sending Members to Parliament, and holding a Court-Leet twice a Year. It stands in *New-land* and *Tinedor* Parishes, is govern'd by a Port-Reeve, and has two Fairs yearly, *viz.* on St. *Francis's* Day, and five Days after *Michaelmas.* It gives Names to the Family of the *Michels,* once possessed of great Demesnes here and in *Devon,* which now belong to the *Rolles,* and spread almost all over *England* ; of which there is one Family at *Kingston* near *Dorchester* in *Devon,* whose Ancestors not long since were Stewards the Princes of *Wales* for their Dutchy of *Cornwal* : And on the East to

Penryn, a Town situate on an Hill, at a little Distance from the Sea, but famous for Markets, having had no less than three every Week, *viz.* on *Wednesdays,* [a] *Fridays,* and *Saturdays.* It is a very pleasant and delightful Place, the Buildings neat, and adorned with fine Gardens and Orchards, insomuch that it seems a Town in a Wood. The Sea clasps it in on both Sides, and affords it a spacious Key. This and other Towns near it drive a considerable Trade in drying and vending Pilchards, to their great Advantage. It is govern'd by a Mayor, Aldermen, and Recorder, which, with the Commoners, chuse Representatives for Parliament. It stands in two Parishes, *viz. Gluvias* and *Roskrow,* and each Part has a Church, of which the first is pretty large, and has many handsome Monuments in it. Most of the Town is in the Parish of *Gluvias,* and there are the Seats of *Alexander Pendarvis* Esq; who has several times been a Member of Parliament for the

---

a   *The* Friday *Market has been disus'd many Years.*

Town, and Mr. *Samuel Ennys*, celebrated for his fine Gardens. In this Place *Walter Bronescomb*, Bishop of *Exeter*, [a] being order'd in a Dream to do it, built a Collegiate Church, which he named *Glasnith* or *Glasseney*, for 13 Prebendaries, some time before 1280. It was a magnificent Building, and had strong Walls and Towers to defend it ; but they now are all fallen to Decay, and there are but small Remains of so stately a Pile. 'Tis also a Borough Town, and sends Members to Parliament. Near this Town is *Arwenack,* the Seat of the famous and ancient Family of the *Killigrews,* of which was Sir *Peter Killigrew,* who, in the Time of *Oliver*'s Usurpation, rode from *Madrid* in *Spain* quite thro' *France,* and having passed the Sea, got to *London* in seven Days. Crossing the Haven, and having passed *St. Maudits,* we come to a Plat of Ground called

Roseland, so named, as some will have it, from a Garden of Roses ; but others imagine it to be so called because it is *Ericetum,* an Heath, as Mr. *Camden* supposes the Word *Ros* in *British* to signify ; but he is mistaken, as 'tis manifest they are, who bear Roses in their Arms, because their Names have *Ros* in them, as *Rosagan, Roscarrocke, Penrose,* &c. for *Ros* or Rose in *Cornish* signifies a Vale or Valley. More inward is

Lanhidrocke, the Seat of the Rt. Hon. *Charles Bodvile Roberts,* Earl of *Radnor,* whose Grandfather *John,* Earl of *Radnor,* was not more eminent at Court for his Abilities in managing State-Affairs, than in his Country for his Generosity and Hospitality, still spoken of by the People here with great Respect.

Going on towards the East from this Vale, the Land

---

[a] Godw. de Præs. 461.

dints in again, and makes a large Bay, called *Trueardaith-Bay*, which signifies a Bay of the Town at the Sand, which receives divers Rivers, of which the chief is that which passes by

Lanladron, whose Lord Sir *Serlo Lanladron* was summoned a Baron to the Parliament, in that Age when the select Men for Wisdom and Worth among the Gentry were called to Parliament, and their Posterity omitted, if defective therein. Those Times, my Author in his Margin tells us, were the Reign of King *Edward* I. Here is an Oak that bears speckled Leaves.

Two Miles from hence the River *Fowey* runs into the Sea, and makes an Haven, which takes its Name from it ; but 'tis called in the *British* Tongue *Foath.* The Town is stretched along up the Sea-Shore, and hath a Market, and sends Members to the Parliament. It is guarded with Block-houses, and fortified with Ordnance. 'Tis at present but a mean Place, but in ancient Times was a considerable Port, and famous for the Bravery and Numbers of the Seamen, who distinguished themselves in Sea-Fights two or three hundred Years ago, as may appear from this Town's bearing a Compound of all the Arms of the Cinque-Ports. King *Edward* IV. built a Fort on each Side of the Harbour ; but being offended with the Inhabitants soon after for plundering some *French* Ships, after he had concluded a Peace with *Lewis* XI. he took from them all their Ships and Naval Stores. The Market here is kept on *Saturdays,* and the Fair   The *Treffries* have long had a Mansion here. On the other Side of the Haven, and over against *Fowey,* stands

Hall, noted for its pleasant Walks on the Side of an Hill. 'Twas anciently the Seat of the *Fitzwilliams,* from whom, by an Heiress, it descended to the *Mohuns*, an ancient and noble Family, descended from the *Mohuns* Earls of *Somerset,* and *Courtney* Earl of *Devonshire,* whose Ancestor seems to be *William de Mohun,* an expert Commander, who accompanied the *Norman* Conqueror in his victorious Army into *England* ; but it being at length sold to the *Keckwich's,* they settled at *Boconocke,* where they had a noble Mansion, till the late Lord *Charles Mohun* was slain in a Duel with Duke *Hamilton, Nov* 15, 1712. by whose Death that Branch of the Family is extinct ; but there are Men of considerable Note of that Name in this County, tho none so nearly related as to inherit the Barony. Higher up the River lies

Lestuthiel, which is supposed to be the *Uzella* of *Ptolomy* ; which Name seems in some part retained, the Word *Lest* being prefixed only to denote its high Situation, for it was situate upon an high Hill, where *Lestormin,* an aged Castle, now stands ; but the Town is now removed into the Valley. In the *British* History 'tis called *Pen Uchel coit, i.e.* An high Mountain in a Wood. Some will have *Exeter* meant by the *Roman Uzella* ; but the Situation assign'd by *Ptolomy,* and the Name it still retains, plainly determine for this Place. It is now a little Town, and not at all populous, because the Chanel of the River *Fowey,* which in the last Age used to carry up the Tide to the very Town, and bring up Vessells of Burthen, is now so stopt by the Sands coming from the Lead-Mines, that it is too shallow for Barges. However, 'tis still a Market and Borough Town, where the County-Court is usually kept, and the Lord Warden of the Stannaries hath his Court, Prison, and Office of Coinage, or stamping their Tin, by the Favour (as the Inhabitants say) of *Edmund* Earl of *Cornwal,* who had his Palace there. In

Mr. *Camden's* Time it might have been the County-Town, as he says ; but *Launceston* is now the Place, where the Assizes are held, and which is commonly accounted the Shire-Town. Its Market is on *Fridays,* and Fair on St. *Bartholomew's* Day. It is appointed by 11 *Henry* VII. to keep the Weights and Measures, and sends Members to Parliament. In this Town there was formerly a Custom, tho' now discontinued, for a Person on *Low Sunday* to act the Part of a King, and in brave Apparel, and finely mounted, with a Sceptre in his Hand, and Sword borne before him, to ride thro' the Town to the Church, and after Divine Service feast his Attendants, being served on the Knees, to represent the Royalties of the Honour of *Cornwal.* In this Place also the Earl of *Essex,* who then commanded an Army for the Parliament, was so surrounded by King *Charles* I. and reduced to such Streights, that his Forces were almost starved, and himself obliged to retire by Water from *Fowey to Plimouth,* in Company of the Lord *Roberts* ; after whose Departure, Major-General *Skippon* coming to a Treaty with the King, agreed, that the Parliament's Troops should lay down their Arms, which was the most glorious Event that happen'd to the King during the whole Course of the Civil Wars. The Decay of this Town may be imputed in some measure to the Neighbourhood of *Leskard* and *Bodmin,* which much eclipse its Glory.

Leskard is a fine Town, and has a good Trade, seated upon an Hill, and famous for a Castle and Market, which is kept on *Saturdays,* and has for its chief Commodity, Leathern Wares, Boots and Shoes, with which it furnishes all the neighbouring Towns. It is a Borough, and sends its Representatives to Parliament. 'Tis encompassed with Woods and Commons, which afford both Profit and Pleasure to the Inhabitants. The Woods furnish them with Fuel and Charcoal ; the Commons feed Multitudes of Sheep, and are much used for Horse-Races. At a small Distance from the Town run the Rivers *Repin* and *Dunmere,* which have each a Bridge over them ; the one falls into the *Fowey,* and the other in *Padstow* Chanel ; but the Glory of it is the noble Seat of the Rt. Hon. the Earl of *Radnor,* before mentioned, which has a fine Park adjoining. Ten Miles West of this Town is

Bodman or *Bodmin* ; in *British, Bosuenna,* and in ancient Charters, *Bodminian.* It is a pretty large Town, being near a Mile in Length, but has been much larger, as the Ruins of some Streets on the North Side of the Town manifestly shew. It is situate between two Hills, but in a very wholesome Air, as the long Lives of the Inhabitants do prove, for ninety Years of Age or more is an usual Length among them, and some exceed a hundred ; so that Mr. *Camden*'s Character of it, [a] that 'tis not very healthful, is either a Mistake, or the Air is amended since his Time. The Church is very spacious, but the Living a Vicaridge, in the Gift of Sir *Edmund Prideaux* Bar. It was much damaged by the Fall of its Spire, thrown down by a violent Tempest in 1699, but is since repaired, all but the Spire. The Market affords Plenty of Corn, Beef, Mutton, *&c.* and formerly was a Staple for Yarn ; but that Trade is much decayed thro' the long continuance of the late War, which brought the Prices so low, as to discour-

---

a   *Mr.* Carew *says, 'tis contagiously seated, and thinks it might be better called* Badham, *from its bad air.*

age the spinning. The Market is kept on *Saturdays,* and Fair *March* 13. 'Tis a Borough, and govern'd by a Mayor and Town-Clerk, assisted with 12 Magistrates and 24 Commoners, who alone have the Privilege of chusing their Representatives for Parliament, and stamping Tin. The Sheriffs Prison for insolvent Debtors is kept in this Town. About the Year 905, when the Discipline of the Church was quite neglected in these Parts, K. *Edward* the Elder, by a Decree from Pope *Formosus,* settled a Bishop's See here, and granting him the Manors of *Pawlton, Lawhitton, St. Germans, Pawton, Pregaer, Penryn,* and *Cargaul,* with a View of Frank-pledge, and all Things belonging to it, but Hue and Cry, obliged him to visit the County of *Cornwal* every Year, in order to reform their Errors ; for before this they resisted the Truth to the utmost of their Power, and would not submit to the Apostolical See. Here was the Bishop's Residence awhile ; but the *Danish* Wars disturbing the Nation, it was translated to *St. Germans,* and after being added to *Kirton* or *Credington* in *Devon,* it was remov'd from thence, and fix'd at *Exeter,* where it now remains. This Town has been principally concerned in two Rebellions, the one of *Perkin Warbeck,* who gather'd Forces here, till he thought himself strong enough to take *Exeter,* and the other in King *Edward* VI's Reign, when the *Cornish* and *Devonshire* Men being rampart, their Major, one *Boyer,* was very active to assist them, and was deservedly hanged for his Pains, but 'twas one of the merriest Executions that ever was ; for Sir *Anthony Kingston,* the Provost-Marshal of the King's Army, who was appointed the Judge of those Rebels, first dined with Mr. Major, and then hang'd him on a Gallows which he had provided, tho' his Miller's Man offer'd to suffer for him, which Sir *Anthony* would not accept, yet hanged him, because it pleas'd him so well, knowing him a Rebel too. The Major had warning to make his Escape from Sir *Anthony* ; but he not regarding it, his Execution could not be avoided, unless Sir *Anthony* would have disobey'd Orders, and endanger'd his own Life. From that time to this, this Town has been always loyal, and were great Sufferers, with the rest of their Countrymen ; in the late Rebellion. In this Town yearly, in the middle of *July*, is a kind of Carnaval kept, Thousands of People coming to see the Sports and Pastimes. King *Charles* II. honour'd it with his Company in his Journey to *Scilly*, and became a Brother of the Society, which it seems derives its Original from the Times before the Conquest. Near this Town, on the East, is

St. Lawrence, where was anciently an House for Lazars or leprous Persons, well endow'd and govern'd : And on the West a Church, formerly called

St. Guerir, which in the *British* signifies a Physician, because King *Alfred*, being at his Devotion here, was recover'd from a Fit of Sickness ; but when *Neotus*, a Man of great Sanctity and Religion, was buried here, he so much eclipsed the Glory of the former Saint, that the Place was soon after called *Neotstow*, i.e. *Neoth's* Place, and now goes by the Name of *St. Neoths*, and the Monks there were termed Clerks of *St. Neoths*. By the *Domesday* Book we learn, that they had pretty large Revenues ; but 'tis so long since they have been alienated, (to be sure before the Reformation) that there is no Remains nor Remembrance of either of them. The Church, as it now stands, is an handsome Building, having many Jewish Traditions painted in the Glass-Windows, which, 'tis supposed, they took from the Jews who traded thither for

Tin. The Explication is preserved in a Book written in the *Cornish* Tongue, and kept in the Publick Library at *Oxford.* Not far from hence, in a Place called

Pennant, in the Parish of *St. Clare,* are two Monuments, the one hollow'd on the Top in the Form of a Chair ; the other is called, The other Half-Stone, and they are thus superscribed :

Thus to be read :

Doniert Rogavit Pro Animâ

Implying, that *Doniert* or *Dungarth,* K. of *Cornwal,* who was drown'd *A.D.* 872, gave that Land to the Religious here for the Good of his Soul.

Near *St. Clare* is an Heap of large Stones, under which lies a great Stone, so like a Cheese, that it seems to be pressed by the others into that Form, and is therefore called *Wring* Cheese. They lie upon a high Rock, and doubtless were accidentally, by Nature, piled one upon another, for they are placed awry, and the least of them lies at the Bottom. Near to these, on the neighbouring Plain, are to be seen a great many Stones, placed in a kind of square Figure, of which seven or eight are at an equal Distance one from the other. They are oblong, rude, and unhewn, pitched in the Ground at one End, standing upon the Down in three Circles, the Centres whereof are in a right Line, and the middlemost Circle is the biggest. The People thereabouts call them *Hurlers*, out of a pious Belief that they were Men turned into Stones for playing at Ball on the *Sunday*. Others will have them to be Trophies in Memory of some Battel fought thereabouts, and others will have them set there for Boundaries, as Authors say, was the usual Way to set out the Limits of Possessions ; but the truest Opinion is, that they were Burying-places of the ancient *Britains*, and fixed for Sepulchral Monuments, as the Stone just before mentioned was, and as the long Stone upon the same Downs, about half a Mile distant from the *Hurlers*, plainly appears to be, by having this Mark on both Sides of it.

On this Coast the River *Loo* opens it self a Passage into the Sea, and there gives Name to two little Towns, joined together by a Stone Bridge, called

Eastlow and *Westlow*. They are neither of them of any Note for Trade ; but *Eastlow* being the later erected, is in the best Condition. They both send Members to Parliament, and are govern'd by a Mayor and Burgesses.

Westlow, which is also called *Port-Pigham*, is a Borough and Market Town, of longer standing than *Eastlow*. 'Twas formerly famous for Fishing ; but now that Trade is wholly laid aside here, and the Town is much decayed. The Markets are on *Saturdays*, and Fair on *April* 24. Near the Mouth is a small Island called *St. George*, where abundance of Sea-Pyes breed. Somewhat Westward from hence lieth

Kilgarth, which was anciently the Seat of the *Bevils*, a Family of especial Note in these Parts for Antiquity and Gentry. It belongs now to the *Kendals*, an ancient Family, whose chief Seat was at *Treworgy*, a Town about three Miles distant.

From hence we meet with nothing remarkable till we come at the little River *Liver*, abounding with Oysters, of a much more grateful Taste than those in the *Tamar*, into which it runs, and pasting by *Minhennead*, (where anciently was an House for Lazars or leprous Persons, which are not uncommon in this Country, thro' eating Fish just taken, or their Livers,) comes to

Pool, so called from its low Situation, where the *Trelawnies* have a large House, and did anciently reside ; but since the Reign of Qu. *Elizabeth*, they have removed their Seat to a Place within two Miles of the River *Loo*, where they have large Possessions, descended to them by a Marriage with one of the Heiresses of the *Courtneys* Earls of *Devonshire*. They are a very ancient Family, and many of them have been long eminent in this Country. We find Sir *John Trelawny* serving as Knight of the Shire in Parliament 1 *Henry* V. and 9 *ejusdem*. The Rt. Rev. Father in God Sir *Jonathan Trelawny*, first Lord Bishop of *Bristol*, then of *Exeter*, and now of *Winchester*, is of this Family, as also Lieutenant-General *Trelawny*, who was late Governor of *Plimouth*. From hence the *Liver* runs to

St. Germans, the greatest Parish in *Cornwal*, and in the last Century populous, being stored with commodious Dwellings for sundry ancient Gentlemen and wealthy Farmers, but now a small Borough Town, which, had it not the Privilege of sending Representatives to Parliament, would be accounted a sorry Village, for the Town consists only of a few Fishermens Cottages, who maintain themselves by fishing in the Sea and neighbouring Rivers. It hath a Fair on *August* 1, and a large Church proportionable to the Parish. But as contemptible a Place as now it is, it was anciently a Bishop's See, and had a famous Monastery in it. In the *Danish* Wars, the Bishop's See, which had been placed at *Bodmin*, was, thro' Fear, removed hither ; but after the Succession of some few Bishops, *Levinus* or *Levingus*, Bishop of *Kirton* in *Devon*, a great Favourite of *Canutus* the *Dane*, obtained a Royal Grant to have it annexed to his own Seat ; but this See also continued not long, being translated soon after to the chief City in those Parts, *Exeter*, where it now remains, yet to the Advantage *of St. Germans*, which was appointed for the Seat to the Suffragan by that Bishop. Here was also a small Monastery, built by *Leofrick* Bishop of *Exeter*, and dedicated to St. *German* of *Antisiodorum* or *Auxerre*, who came into *Britain* to suppress the *Pelagian* Heresy.

At the end of this Town stands an House of the ancient Bishops, and in the Parish lieth *Bake*, the Mansion of the *Moyls* ; *Keverel*, the Seat of the *Langdons* ; and near it *Tregonnocke*, the ancient Seat of the *Smiths*.

Upon this River also stands *Trematon* Castle, if an Heap of Ruins may deserve that Name, for we find nothing else here ; tho' we understand by *Domesday*-Book, that *William* Earl of *Moriton* had a Castle and Market here. It serves for a Prison for such Persons as have committed Capital Crimes within the Compass of the Lordship, and the Keeper has a poor House in it ; and the Earls, afterwards Dukes of *Cornwal*, had a Barony in these Parts, of which this Place was the Head, as we learn from the Inquisitions.

A little below this Town stands *Shevroke*, the Seat and Inheritance of the *Daunies*, by whose Daughter and Heiress it descended to the Earls of *Devon*. They built the Church, and two Knights of the Name lie buried in it. Their Pictures are embossed on their Tombs.

At a little Distance from hence the *Liver* empties it self into the *Tamar*, which divides this County from *Devonshire*, where, near the Mouth, we find

Saltash or *Saltesse*, about five Miles from *Plimouth*, which is on the other Side of the *Tamar*. 'Twas in ancient Times called *Esse*, and belonged then to the Family of the *Valtorts*, who had such large Possessions in these Parts, that in the 5th Year of King *John*, *Roger de Valtort* answer'd for 59 Knights Fees to the Honour of *Moriton*. 'Tis now a populous trading Town, govern'd by a Mayor and nine Aldermen, and has a Market every *Saturday*, and a Fair on St. *James*'s Day. 'Tis pretty well stored with Merchants, and enjoys a great many Privileges over the whole Haven, *viz.* a yearly Rent of all Boats and Barges belonging to it. Anchorage for Ships, crowning dead Persons, laying Arrests, *&c.* When the Lord *Mohun* in the late Civil Wars took this Town for the King, he found in it ten Pieces of Ordnance, 700 Men in Arms, and a Ship of 16 Guns in the Port, which shew'd that 'twas a considerable Place, and drove a foreign Trade. It sends Burgesses to Parliament. From this Town there is a Passage by a Ferry over to *Devonshire*, called *The Crimble Passage*, which is very dangerous when the Wind is boisterous. Not far from hence runs out the Neck of Land called,

Mount-Edgecomb, the Seat of the ancient Family of the *Edgecombs*, pleasantly situated in the midst of a Park, and having a fine Prospect of the winding Haven under it. It was made a Garrison for King *Charles* I. against the Parliament ; but upon the Restoration of K. *Charles* II. so well recover'd its Lustre, that when that King gave Sir *Richard Edgecomb* a Visit in his Voyage to *Plimouth*, he much commended the lovely Situation of his Mansion. *Richard Edgecomb* Esq; a Gentleman who has for several Parliaments been Burgess for *Plimpton* in *Devon*, is present Lord of this fair Estate and Seat. This Town, and great Part of the Parish of *Maker*, tho' they are on the *Cornish* Side of *Tamar*, are in *Devonshire* : But as to the Ecclesiastical Jurisdiction, they are in the Archdeaconry of *Cornwal*, and so some Tracts of Land on *Devonshire*-Side are belonging to *Cornwal.* How this came to pass, 'tis loss of Time to conjecture. Near *Mount-Edgcomb* is the Parish of

Rame, and the Neck of Land called *Ram-head*, which was formerly a Gentleman's Seat, but now is known chiefly to Mariners and Seamen for a little vaulted Chapel, which standing on the top of the Promontory, is a Sea-mark, but more particularly for the Loss of the *Coronation*, a Second Rate Man of War, which was sunk here, and 500 Men in her. The Cellars hereabouts fetch great Rents at the Time of Pilchard-Fishing for curing those Fish. 'Twas anciently called *Tamarworth*. More Northward is

Anthony, eminent only for its Lords of the Family of *Carew,* and for its Neatness and Fish-pond, which lets in the Sea, and furnishes the Inhabitants with Plenty of Fish, which are so tame, that they come to a certain Place every Evening to be fed, and at any time will be called together by a Noise like chopping their Meat, which shews that Fish can hear. Near this Place is

Milbrooke, now called *Meloch,* a pretty Town for the Fishing Trade, which hath also in former Days furnished our Fleet with many able Soldiers. Here was a Woman deliver'd of two Male Children at ten Weeks distance, and both lived.

The Southern Coast having been thus survey'd, we will now go to the North, and beginning again at the Land's-End, pass along the Shore, yet not neglecting any Inland Towns of Note that lie in our way, and so the first we meet with is

St. Jies, or (as it is vulgarly but corruptly called) *St. Ives.* The Coast from the Land's-End to this Town is a long Tract of sandy Banks. It took its Name from an *Irish* Female Saint, named *Jia,* and hangs over the Sea like a little Tongue. It was formerly called *Pendinas,* and the Haven below, which receives the River *Hail* into it, is therefore called by the Seamen St. *Jies* Bay. 'Tis now an inconsiderable Place, because the Bay, which might open a Way to Trade, lying exposed to the North-West Wind, called by Mr. *Somner, Caurus,* is so stuffed up with Sand, that the People have been forced to remove more than once. Their only Trade, and that a poor one too is with *Cornish* Slates ; but they enjoy the like Privilege with their neighbouring Boroughs of sending Members to Parliament. The Cliffs hereabouts have some Streaks of a glittering Metal like Copper, of which Mines are found hereabouts. Here also stood the Watch-Tower mentioned by *Orosius*, opposite to another in *Gallicia*.

The small Isle of *Gudreny* lies at the Entrance of this Haven, on the West Side ; and a little farther, but about three Miles within Land, stands

Redruth, a Town of more Resort than *St. Ives*, tho' no Sea-Port. 'Tis a Town of no great Antiquity, nor doth it afford any thing remarkable, no more than the rest of the Coast, till we come to

Trerice, the Seat of the Lord *Arundel*, called of *Trerice*, to distinguish him from another Branch of the same Family, the Lord *Arundel* of *Wardour*. This Family came into *England* with the Conqueror, and this Branch have bean seated in this Town, ever since King *Edward* III.'s Time, by Marriage with the Family of *Trere* or *Trerice*, being eminent for their Services to their King and Country, for which they were at length rewarded with this honourable Title of Baron, *viz.*

Sir *John Arundel* Kt. was Vice-Admiral to King *Henry* VII. and VIII. and took *Duncan Campbel*, the famous *Scotch* Pirate, Prisoner in a Sea-Fight. His Son *John Arundel* was Knight of the Shire for this County in divers Parliaments, and tho' near 80 Years of Age when the Parliament took up Arms against King *Charles* I. he valiantly defended *Pendennis* Castle against their Forces a long time. He lost two Sons in those unhappy Wars, but left for his Heir

Richard Arundel, who attended the said King in Person, and was a Commander in his Army. He had one of the best Estates of any Gentleman in *Cornwal*, but lost it by adhering to his Sovereign, who had no other way to reward his Merit, but with the Dignity of a Baron, which King *Charles* II. conferred on him *March* 23, 1664. He has been succeeded by his Son and Grandson of the same Name ; which last hath left

John, now Lord *Arundel* of *Trerice*, for his Heir. He is a Minor, being born *Nov.* 21, *A.D.* 1701.

Here the Country begins to grow wider on both Coasts ; and advancing farther, we meet with a little Chapel dedicated to *S. Pyranus*, an *Irish* Saint, who was buried here. The Legend magnifies his Sanctity, by attributing incredible Miracles to him, *viz.* feeding ten *Irish* Kings and their Armies eight Days with the Flesh of three Cows only, and raising not only Men from the Dead, but Hogs, *&c.* A little more from the Shore lies

St. Colombs, a little Market-Town, with a Church, consecrated to the Memory of St. *Columba*, and not *Columbus* the *Scotsman*, as some learned Men have thought. It has a Market on *Saturdays*, and two Fairs *April* 24, and *June* 11. 'Tis the Lordship of the *Lanheron Arundels*, many of whom lie buried in the Church there, which is in their Patronage. Nearer the Coast stands

Lanheron, another Seat of the *Arundels* Knights, who (upon the Account of their vast Riches) did of old bear the Name of the Great *Arundels*. Their Name is *French* ; for in that Tongue, *Hirondelle* signifies a Swallow, and their Name in Latin is written, *De Hirundine*, which their Arms confirm, being in a Field *Sable* six Swallows *Argent.* One of this Family was very famous for his Courage and Conduct in the *French* Wars. They are since promoted to the Dignity of Barons, by the Name of Lord *Arundel* of *Wardour*-Castle in *Wiltshire*. The Father of the present Lord was one of those five Lords who lay so long in the Tower for the Popish Plot against King *Charles* II. and was made a Minister of State by King *James* II. His Brother *Thomas* was slain at the Battle on the *Boyne*, fighting for the said King. At a small Distance from hence there is a Hill, which has a Rampire on the top of it, and a Causey leading to it. 'Tis called, *Castellan Danis, i.e.* the *Danes* Camp, because that People, when they prey'd upon the *English* Coasts, encamped here, as they did in other Places of the Country. Farther Eastward rises the River *Alan*, or *Combalan*, commonly called *Camel*, from its winding Chanel, (*Cam* in *Cornish* signifying Winding) which running gently into the *Severn* Sea, presents us with a little Market Town, called

Padstow, or *Petrockstow, i.e. Petrock's* Place. It takes the Name from one *Petrocus,* a *British* Saint, who lived here in a religious manner. His Tomb or Shrine was remaining in the E. Side of the Church in [a] *Leland's* Time. It was called before *Loderick* and *Laffenac,* and afterwards *Adelstow,* i.e, *Athelstan's* Place, because King *Athelstan is* looked upon as the chief Donor of its Privileges ; but *Patrockstow,* now contracted into *Padstow,* is the Name that has long prevail'd. It purchas'd the Privilege of a Corporation in or near the last Century. 'Tis a Sea port, tho a bad one, and lies convenient for an *Irish* Trade, being but 24 Hours easy Sail. The ancient Family of *Prideaux* have a stately Mansion-House like a Castle here, built not long before Mr. *Camden's* Time. The Mar-

---

a   Lel. Itin. Vol II

ket is on *Saturdays,* and the Fairs on

About five Miles from *Padstow,* on the Chanel, stands

Wadbridge, a Town which takes the Name from the remarkable Bridge there over the River, being much the largest in the County. It has 17 Arches, and was built by *Nicholas Lovebone,* Vicar of the Place, to prevent the Dangers which Passengers were exposed to by ferrying over the Chanel. The Foundation of some of the Arches is upon Woolpacks, because they could find nothing but Quicksands to build on. Near this Place are nine Cones and great Stones, called the Sisters, standing in a Rank, but why is not known. The Town has a Market every *Saturday,* and a Fair on   Near the Rise of the *Camel,* we meet a little Market and Borough Town, taking its Name from it, and called

Camelford, which some write *Gaffelford. Leland* tells us, its ancient Name was *Kemblan,* and that *Arthur,* the *English* Hector, was slain here ; which, if true, his Birth and Death happen'd near the same Place ; but if that be doubted, Tradition assures us of a bloody Battel fought here between the *Saxons* and *Britains* about the Year of Christ 820, which *Marianus* confirms. It hath a Market on *Fridays,* and a Fair on St. *Thomas's* Translation, *July 7.*

Near *Camelford* was S. *Nunns-Pool,* now called *Allernon,* where Madmen were cur'd by plunging and dowsing them in it.

A little farther on the Coast stands *Tindagel,* in Latin *Tindagium,* where 'tis said *Arthur* was born. Its Situation is part of it on a Slip of Land like a little Tongue, and part upon an Island, which in ancient Times was joined to the main Land by a Bridge. Nothing is now left of it but the splendid Ruins of an ancient Castle, which shews it was impregnable, because it is built on an huge Rock. One *John Northampton,* Mayor of *London,* was imprison'd here for Life for some great Misdemeanor. It would but abuse the Readers Patience to relate the Story of *Uter Pendragon,* who, by *Merlin's* Art, assumed the Shape of *Gorlois,* a Prince of *Wales,* and begat *Arthur* of his Wife. 'Tis one of *Jeffrey's* Fables. Upon the same Coasts appears

Botereaux Castle, now contracted into *Boscastel,* being built by the *Botereauxes,* who were the Lords of it. Their Arms are in a Shield *Argent* three Toads *Sable,* no dishonourable Coat, because the Kings of *France* had the same Arms before they assumed the Lillies. The first Men of Note among them was *William Botereaux,* who married *Alicia,* the Daughter of Sir *Robert Corbet,* who was Sister to *Henry I's* Mistress, the Mother of *Reginald* Earl of *Cornwal.* He had eleven Successors to him in the right Line, who, by their intermarrying with the *Moyls, St. Laud* or *St. Lo's,* and *Thwengs,* wealthy Families, had got a mighty Estate in these Parts : But *Margaret,* the only Daughter and Heiress to the last, carried the Estate by Marriage to the *Hungerfords,* from whom it descended to the *Hastings,* who enjoyed the Castle till Queen *Elizabeth's* Reign. The Market here is kept on *Thursdays,* and Fair on

This County hitherto has been but narrow, but now it enlarges it self, and is become above 30 Miles broad, (tho' Mr. *Camden* says but 23.) *Stow,* the Seat of the ancient Family of the *Granvilles,* stands in the widest Part

; but Sir *John Granville,* who was employed by King *Charles* II. in many important Negociations, in order to his Restauration, was the first that bore the Dignity of Peerage, being created Baron of *Kilkhampton* and *Biddiford,* Viscount *Lansdown,* and Earl of *Bath,* (of which Family we shall speak more fully in its place.) He built himself a stately Palace here, which is esteemed the finest in these Western Parts of *England,* tho' he had before four good Seats, *viz.* at *Wolstan, Stanbury, Clifton,* [a] and *Lanow.* South-West of *Stow,* near the *Tamar,* stands

Stratton, a little Market-Town, noted chiefly for Gardens and Garlick. The chief Commodity, besides their Orchards of that Hundred, is Countryman's Treacle. 'Twas here that Sir *Ralph Hopton,* who commanded the King's Forces, fought Major-General *Chudleigh,* who had before defeated Sir *Bevil Granville's* Party, for the Parliament, *May* 16, 1643. and defeated him, taking him Prisoner. For this Service, Sir *Ralph* was made a Lord, by the Title of Baron *Stratton,* at *Oxford, Sept.* 4, 1644. with remainder to Sir *Arthur Hopton* Kt. his Uncle, and his Heirs Male ; but they both died without such Heirs, and so the Honour became extinct. In the Place where this Battel was fought, there follow'd a prodigious Crop of Barley, of 10 or 12 Ears on a Stalk. The Market is on *Tuesdays,* and Fair on   Near this Place is

Lancells, where the Family of the *Chaumonds* had a Seat in Mr. *Camden's* Time, new built ; but now 'tis extinct, which may seem strange, when 'tis said, that [b] one of that Family was Uncle and Great Uncle ; to 300

---

a *Where is a neat Seat belonging to one of the* Arundels of Trerice *by a younger Branch.*

b *He was 60 Years Justice of the Peace, and lived to see the youngest of five Sons and Daughters 40 Years old.*

Persons at least. Here was a Cell to the Abbey of *Hart-land.*

The *Tamar* rises in this Part of the County near the Northern Shore, and runs quite cross to the South, having many Towns situate on its Shore, of which these are most remarkable, *viz.*

Tamarton, called by *Ptolomy, Tamara.* The ancient Family of *Trevilians,* who much increased their Estate by Marriages with the Families of *Walesborough* and *Raleigh* of *Nettlestead,* had their Seat in this Place. Here was a leaden Coffin taken up, with the Body of an ancient Duke of this County, who had been buried 500 Years ; but as soon as it was touched, it moulder'd to Dust. The River gliding from hence, is increased by several Rivulets, (upon one of which stands *Penhall,* formerly a Lordship of the Earls of *Huntingdon,* but now of the *Granvilles,)* which discharge themselves into it, and then comes to

Launceston, or (as 'tis vulgarly called) *Launston.* 'Tis a Market, Mayor, and Borough Town, the usual Place for publick Business, for the Assizes and County-Gaol are usually kept, and Elections of Knights of the Shire made, here. [a] In ancient Writings it is called *Dunhurd,* and *Lan-stuphadon, i.e.* The Church of St *Stephen.* It is a neat Place, situate on a rising Ground, and including the two Towns of *Dunevet* and *Newport,* which last still retains the Privilege of sending Members to Parliament. *William* Earl of *Moriton* built a strong [b] Castle here, and a Col-

---

a   *The Statute of* 32 Henry VIII. *endowed this Town with the Privilege of a Sanctuary ; but we find not that it was used. Queen* Elizabeth *founded a Free-School here, and endowed it with a competent Pension.*

b   *King* Richard I *gave this Castle to Earl* John, *his Brother, afterwards King* John, *who committed the Custody of it to* Richard Revet, *Governor of* Exeter *Castle, which was also his. It was called* Castle-terrible, *because of its* legiate Church for Prebendaries, as appears from *Domes-day*-Book, where it is called *Launsteveton,* because it was dedicated to St. *Stephen. Reginald* Earl of *Cornwal,* about the Year 1150, tho' then vehemently opposed by the Bish-ops of *Exeter,* converted it into a Monastery, as Mr. *Camden* says ; but the Author of the Additions to *Camden* says, That it was *William* (which should be *Robert*) *War-lewast,* Bishop of *Exeter,* who settled the best part of the College-Lands on it, but kept the Residue to himself. The Lord *Hopton* was forced to disband his Army in this Place by General *Fairfax,* and so the Parliament-Forces seemed to recover the Disgrace they had suffer'd in these Parts under the Earl of *Essex.* The Market at *Launceston* is on *Saturdays,* and the Fairs on *May* 1, *June* 24, and on St. *Leonard's* Day ; but *Newport* has neither Market nor Mayor. At *St. Thomas,* by this Town, was an House for Lazars. The River leads us next by an high Mountain, which is stretched out a great way in length, called by *Marianus,*

Henᵹeꞃ-ðoun, and by the *Saxon* Annals, Henᵹiꞃꞇeꞃ ðun, *i.e. Hengist's-Hill,* now called *Heng-ston Hill,* a Place anciently so rich in Veins of Tin, that the Country-People have a Proverb in Rhyme :

Hengston-down well ywrought,

Is worth London *dear ybought.*

But now they are worn out, yet Plenty of *Cornish* Dia-monds are found here, which will never occasion such a Proverb. A Cloud sitting on this Hill, foreshews Rain

Strength.

soon. It was at this Hill that the *Cornish Britains,* who had joined with the *Danes* to infest *Devonshire,* and drive out the *Saxons,* were forced to a Battel by King *Egbert* ; and being worsted, were almost all of them cut to pieces. This happen'd about the Year 831, and 'tis probable the Hill then received the *Saxon* Name of *Hengist's-Hill,* from *Hengist,* their first Leader into *Britain.* Beneath this Town, the *Tamar* passes by

Halton, the Habitation anciently of the *Rouses,* the Lords of *Little Modbury* in *Devon,* from whom, by an Heiress, it hath descended to the *Dimocks* : From whence we come to the River's Mouth, where we find *Saltash,* which having before observed, we must conclude our Survey, and shall now proceed to give an Account of those honourable Persons who have been

The EARLS *and* DUKES *of* Cornwal, *viz.*

Robert de Moriton, Brother to the Conqueror by the Mother's Side, who gave him this Earldom soon after his Settlement, with 793 Manors. He left by *Maud* his Wife,

William, the Heir of his Honour and Estate. He being disgusted with King *Henry* I because he deny'd him the Earldom of *Kent,* of which he supposed himself to be the legal Heir, Bishop *Odo,* his Uncle, dying without Heirs, he fled into *Normandy,* and there joined with *Robert* Duke of *Normandy* to recover *England* from *Henry,* who was his younger Brother ; but *Robert* being conquer'd, Earl *William* was taken Prisoner, and, with his Liberty, lost his Honours ; of which being deprived, he became a Monk of *Bermondsey* in *Surrey,* where he died.

His Earldom of *Moriton* this King gave to *Stephen* Earl of *Blois* ; but that of *Cornwal* was given to

Reginald de Dunstanvil, his natural Son by a Daughter of Sir *Robert Corbet,* by K. *Stephen, 5 Reg.* 1140. This Earl left no legitimate Issue ; whereupon K. *Henry* II. took the Earldom into his Hands, with all his Lands in *England* and *Wales,* which he gave not long after to his youngest Son,

John, who was at that time but nine Years of Age, whose Brother *Richard* I. confirmed it to him, and gave him several Other large Revenues. Earl *John* held it till he was King, and then he granted to *Henry Fitzcount,* an illegitimate Son of Earl *Reginald,* but a Person of Merit, the whole County of *Cornwal,* with the Demesnes, and all its Appurtenances, to farm, until the King was satisfied whether be ought to hold it by Right of Inheritance ; but at the same time, or near it, the said King made his Son,

Richard, Earl of *Cornwal,* whom also his Brother K. *Henry* III. created Earl of *Poictou.* He was a very powerful Prince, and thought to be the richest Person in *Europe,* except crown'd Heads. He was very religious, according to those Times, building and endowing divers Monasteries and Churches, and taking upon him two Expeditions to the Holy Land, to rescue it out of the Hands of the *Saracens,* where he gave such Proofs of his Courage and Skill in Military Affairs, as he did also in *Gascoigne* against the King of *France,* that the Pope offer'd him the Kingdom of *Naples,* and the seven Electors of *Germany* chose him Emperor, which last he accepted, and was crown'd at *Aix-la-Chapelle A. D.* 1257. But the Elector of *Bavaria* and some other Princes turning his Enemies, he grew so uneasy, that he left his Dignity, and a great Part of his Treasure, and returned into *England,* where he died soon after, and was buried in his Abbey of *Hales* near *Winchcombe* in *Gloucestershire.* To him succeeded

Edmund, his Son, in this Earldom. He married *Margaret,* the Daughter of *Gilbert de Clare,* Earl of *Gloucester* ; but dying without Issue, (28 *Edw.* I.) the King seiz'd his Honour and Estate, and allowing his Widow 500*l,* a Year out of it for Life, gave all the rest to his Son the Prince, who was afterwards King *Edward* II. and so this Honour was for some Years suspended, till *Edward* II. coming to the Throne, gave it to

Pierre Gaveston, a *Gascoigner,* who had gotten his Favour not by any Merit, but by his Vices ; but he being render'd odious to the Nobility by his Crimes, and particularly for debauching the Prince, was seiz'd by them, and beheaded ; whereupon the Earldom was conferred on

John de Eltham, second Son of *Edward* II. by his Brother King *Edward* III. He died young and unmarried ; whereupon the said King erected it into a Dukedom, and invested his Son,

Edward, surnamed the Black Prince, an accomplished Soldier, with the Titles of Prince of *Wales,* (which the *Welch* consented to) Duke of *Aquitain* and *Cornwal,* and Earl of *Chester,* by putting a Wreath on his Head, a Ring on his Finger, and a Verge or Rod into his Hand ; ever since which Time it has been settled and agreed, That the eldest Son of the King, who is Heir to the Crown, shall be Earl of *Cornwal,* and by a special Act of Parliament made in that Case, he is presumed to be of Age as soon as he is born, so that he may claim Livery and Seisin of the said Dukedom the same Day he is born,

and ought by Right to obtain it, as if he had fully com-
pleated the Age of 21 Years : Yet

Richard de Bourdeaux, eldest Son of the Black
Prince, was not Duke of *Cornwal* by Virtue of the former
Law or Settlement, because he was not eldest Son of the
King, but his Grandson, and therefore he was created by
a particular Patent : But

Henry, the eldest Son of K. *Henry* IV.

Henry, the eldest Son of K. *Henry* V.

Edward, the eldest Son of K. *Henry* VI.

Edward, the eldest Son of K. *Edward* IV.

Edward, the eldest Son of K. *Richard* III.

Arthur, the eldest Son of K. *Henry* VII.

Were all Dukes of *Cornwal* successively according to
the Act ; but

Henry, the second Son of *Henry* VII. was created
Duke of *Cornwal* after his Brother *Arthur's* Decease ; yet

Edward, the eldest Son of K *Henry* VIII.

Henry, the eldest Son of K. *James* I.

Were by Birth Dukes of *Cornwal* ; but

Charles, the second Son of K. *James* I. was created
after Prince *Henry's* Death.

Charles, the eldest Son of K. *Charles* I. was born
Duke of *Cornwal* ; but

George, now Prince of *Wales,* and Duke of *Cornwal,*
was created by Patent.

Men of an inferior Rank, but of Eminency in their Stations, may follow these Nobles, because greatest Benefactors to the Publick, and Credit to their Country, of which this County has produced some, *viz.*

Sir *Richard Edgcomb* Sen. Comptroller of the Houshold and Privy Counsellor to King *Henry* VII. by whom he was sent in divers Embassies.

Sir *Thomas Arundel,* a younger Brother of *Lanhearn-House,* who married Q. *Katherine Howard,* and was a Privy Counsellor to King *Edward* VI.

Arthur, King of *Britain* by Succession, a great Christian Hero.

Richard Carew Esq, who wrote a Survey of this County, of whom Mr. *Camden* thus speaks ; "That he was no less eminent for his honourable Ancestors, than his own Virtue and Learning." And to whom he says, "He was beholden in writing his *Britannia* for some Directions." His History was dedicated to Sir *Walter Raleigh.*

Michael Blasinpain, a Poet, who lived in King *Edward* III's Reign.

John Skuish, a Person so favour'd by Cardinal *Wolsey,* that he made him one of his Cabinet Council. He wrote a Chronicle, and a Treatise *de Bello Trojano.* 'Tis thought he favour'd the Reformation.

Sir *John Tregonwell,* Founder of a Family of that Name in *Dorsetshire,* where he will be mentioned again, tho' himself was of this County. He was a great Civilian.

Sir *William Lower,* a tolerable Poet in King *Charles* I.'s Reign.

Sir *John Elliot,* a famous Speech-maker.

Francis Rous Esq; Speaker of *Oliver's* Parliament, and Provost of *Eaton*-College.

And since Mr. *Carew* has thought fit to mention them in his History, we may add

Ralph Hayes, a Blacksmith, and

Mr. *Atwell,* Parson of *St. Tue* :

Both of them much talked of for their Success (which is above Skill) in the Practice of Physick. This last was a learned Man in his own Profession, and not unskilled in Physick. His Judgment in Urines almost equalled the most skilful in that Profession. He was very successful with common Remedies. He attended the Poor *gratis,* and the Rich for little Fees, which he gave usually half to the Servants, and the rest, with his Benefice, to pious Uses ; so that his Virtue and Goodness was admir'd by all, and loved by most that knew him.

William Noy Esq; Attorney-General in King *Charles* I.'s Days. His Character is sufficiently blazon'd in our Historians. He was a Native here.

The ancient and honourable Houses of *Arundel* and *Granville* have produced several Heroes, famous for their Achievements both by Land and Sea, as *Thomas Arundel,* who signaliz'd himself so much in *Hungary* against the *Turks,* that the Emperor *Rodolph* II. made him a Count of the Empire.

Sir *John Arundel,* Vice-Admiral to the Kings *Henry* VII. and VIII. and his Son, who so bravely defended *Pen-dennis* Castle above mentioned.

Sir *Richard Granville* Kt. who lost his Life in a

bloody Fight with the *Spaniards* near the *Tercera* Islands.

Sir *Bevil Granville,* who with unparallel'd Courage encounter'd the Rebels against K *Charles* I. and was slain in the Battel of *Lansdown,* and his Son,

John, who went on in his Father's Steps, and not only maintained King *Charles* I.'s Right in several Battels, and attended his Majesty King *Charles* II. in his Exile, but was one of the most active in his Restoration ; for which Services he was created, *April* 20, 1661. Baron of *Kilkhampton* and *Biddiford,* Viscount *Lansdown,* and Earl of *Bath.*

Sir *Richard Cheverton* is the only Lord Mayor of *London* which was a Native of this County, which we may suppose to proceed from the Distance from thence.

Mr. *Carew* thinks old *Veal* of *Bodmin* deserves a Place here, who, without a Teacher, was very skilful in all manner of Handicraft-Trades ; yea, was a Physician, Surgeon, and Chymist.

BARONETS of this County, *viz*

R *Eginald Mohun,* of *Boconnock,* (*English* Baron) created *Nov.* 25, 1612.

Sir *Richard Roberts, of Truro,* Kt. (*English* Earl) created *July* 13, 1621.

Sir *William Wray,* of *Trebich,* Kt. created *June* 30, 1628.

John Trelawney, of *Trelawney,* Esq; created *July* I, 1628.

Sir *Richard Granville* Kt. younger Brother of Sir *Bevil Granville* Kt. created *April* 9, 1630.

Richard Carew, of *Anthony,* Esq; created *August* 9, 1641. 17 *Car.* I.

William Smith, of *Crantock,* Esq; created *September* 17, 1642. 18 *Car.* I.

Sir *Richard Vivian,* of *Trelowren,* Kt. created *February* 12, 1644. 20 *Car.* I.

William Killigrew, of *Arwynike,* Esq; with remainder to *Peter Killigrew,* of *Arwynike,* aforesaid, Esq; Son of Sir *Peter Killigrew* Kt. created *Dec.* 22, 1660. 12 *Car.* II.

William Godolphin, of *Godolphin,* Esq; created *April* 29, 1661. 13 *Car.* II.

John Coriton, of *Newton,* Esq; created *February* 27, 1661. 14 *Car.* II.

John St. Aubin, of *Clowence,* Esq; created *December* 11, 1671. 23 *Car.* II.

Hender Molesworth, of *Spring Garden,* in *Com. Midd.* Esq; with remainder to his eldest Brother Sir *John Molesworth* of *Pencarrow,* created *July* 19, 1689.

The NATURAL HISTORY *of this County.*

THis County is situate in the 50th Deg. 30 Min. N. Lat. and 6 Deg. of Longitude. The Air being cleansed with frequent Winds and the Tides ; is very pure and healthful, so that the Inhabitants are rarely troubled with any infections Diseases ; yet being sharp and piercing, such as have been sick, especially Strangers, recover but slowly. The Seasons of the Year are something different from those in other Parts ; the Spring is more backward, the Summer more temperate, Autumnal Fruits later, their Harvest rarely being ripe enough for the Barn till near *Michaelmas,* but then well digested, and the Winter, by reason of the warm Breezes, much milder, for they have Frost and Snow but very seldom, and then they soon vanish. Nevertheless the Country being surrounded with the Sea, is subject to such violent Storms, that not only uncover their Houses, but rend up their Hedges, and hinder the Growth of their Trees. One kind of them, which they count most furious, they call a Flaw or Flagh.

The Soil is for the most part mountainous, cover'd with a thin Coat of Earth, and rocky underneath, which renders it hard to be cultivated, and in dry Years unfruitful, yet their Valleys produce Plenty of Grass ; and the Land near the Sea-Shore, which is beautified with many good Towns, being manur'd with a sort of Sea-Weed which they call *Orewood,* and a fat kind of Sea-Sand, yields considerable Quantities of Corn. The middle Part of the Shire, unless it be about some few Towns, lies waste and open ; the Earth is of a blackish Colour, and bears only Heath and spiry Grass, which serves to feed young Cattle.

From the Surface we shall pass to the inner Parts of the Earth, where are found divers Sorts of Stones and Metals. As to the Stones, the Moor-stone is the chief, so called because it is found in Moors and waste Grounds, where it is discover'd either lying upon the Ground, or very little under it. It is of a whitish Colour, and contains in it many glimmering Sparkles. It is of great Use for Buildings, and facing Windows, Doors and Chimneys ; and tho' it requires much Toil in working and framing, because of its Hardness, yet it recompenseth the Charge and Labour, by its withstanding that sharp Weather, which frets even Iron Bars. Here are also other Stones found, as the *Pantuan,* which resembles a grey sort of Marble ; it is digged out of the Sea-Cliffs : *Caraclouse,* which is a Stone as black as Jet ; and Free-stone dug up in the Inland Quarries. For covering their Houses, they have three Sorts of Slate, called by the Inhabitants Heal- ing-Stones, *viz.* the Blue, the Sage-Leaf, and the Grey, which are generally found under another kind of Slate, which they use for Walls. Of these they have such Plenty, that they make a considerable Gain of them, in selling them to their Neighbours, and transporting them into the farther Parts of *Britain* and the *Netherlands.* They have also another sort of Marble Stone, which they make Lime of by fierce Fires made with Furze. Here are also found (as the Writers of the History of this County report) some kinds of Precious Stones, as Diamonds naturally cut and polish'd, but dark and soft ; Pearls, but neither round nor orient, tho' large ; Agates and white Coral ; but none of them being of any great Worth, or in considerable Quantities, they are of as little Use as Profit. On the Sea-Shore also a sort of Pebbles, useful for paving their Yards and Streets, is found.

The Metals which are found here are Copper, Silver, of which 'tis said that the Kings *Edward* I. and III. made a considerable Advantage, and Gold, of which the Workers in the Tin Mines are said to find some little Grains among the Ore ; but the Advantage redounding by these has been so inconsiderable, that all Endeavours after them is laid aside, and the Inhabitants apply themselves wholly to the finding, digging, working and selling of Tin, with which the whole Country, both Hills and Valleys, abounds ; and by reason of its general Use both at home and abroad tor Houshold-Vessels, a gainful Trade is maintained. We can give but a short Account of the Metal it self, and the Ways of managing it, in this small Volume ; and such as desire a large Relation, may consult the Philosophical Transactions, where the most exact Enquiries have been made into both, and ingeniously represented. It is made of little black Stones, lying upon the Surface of the Earth, which they call *Shoad,* because they imagine it to be shot from the main Load or Body of the Mine. Where the Tinners find these Stones, they go to work, and according as the Place is, make one of the two sort of Works, *viz.* Streamworks in low Places, whither they imagine, (but without Ground) that *Noah's* Flood retiring from the Earth, and carrying with it the Rocks and Ground, removed much of the Load from its natural Situation, and scatter'd it here and there in the Valleys and Rivers where it passed : (These Veins of Tin they trace by Ditches to carry off the Water, which would otherwise break in upon them :) Or Load-works upon higher Grounds, in which they sink Holes called Shaffs to a vast

Depth in the Mountains, and work by undermining. In both kinds they shew a wonderful Art and Ingenuity, as well in draining the Waters, and reducing them to one Chanel, as in supporting up their Pits. The Shoad and Load resembles its Bed, and is diversified into reddish, blackish, dusky, and other Colours. After it is brought above Ground in the Stone, it is first broken in pieces with Hammers, and then carried to the Stamping-Mill. If the Stones be over moist, they are dry'd by the Fire in any Iron Grate. From the Stamping-Mill it is carried to the Crazing Mill, where it is bruised to a fine Sand, and then being washed, is sent to the Blowing-House, where it is melted and run into Pigs of about 300 or 400 Weight, some of a finer Nature, called the White, and others of a coarser Sort, called Black Tin, the Owner's Name being set upon every one of them. Lastly, it is carried to the Coining-House, where it is weighed, tasted, *i.e.* try'd whether it be soft or hard, and being stamped with the Dutchy Stamp, the Price is set, and so it is left to the Owner to sell, except the King or Duke have a mind to buy it, for they have the Right of Pre-emption, and may not be refused.

Towns having the special Privilege of the Coinage are, *Helston, Truro, Lestwithiel,* and *Leskard* ; but since Mr. *Camden's* Time, *Pensance* is made a Coinage-Town. *Bodmin* enjoy'd that Privilege in the Reign of King *Edward* I. but lost it in his Son's Time, and the Times for it are *Midsummer* and *Michaelmas* ; but because it happens that all Persons can't have their Tin ready at those Times, others are appointed for Post-Coinage, as they call it, *viz.* at *Lady day* and *Christmas* ; but then they pay 4*d. per* Hundred for the Stamp.

How long these Mines have been discover'd, is uncertain ; but it appears from *Diodorus Siculus* and *Timæus,* that the *Britains* wrought in them, and 'tis thought an Argument, that the *Romans* made some Advantage by them, from a Brass Coin of the Emperor *Domitian,* which was found in these Works ; but the *Saxons* don't seem to hive meddled with them, nor was any great Profit made of them, till *Richard,* Brother of K. *Henry* III. being made Earl of *Cornwal,* gave Encouragement to the Tinners by his Countenance and Contributions, whereby he not only raised to himself vast Revenues, but gave the Inhabitants a clearer Insight into the Profits which might be made of them. These Times much favoured this Manufacture ; for the Mines of Tin in *Spain* being shut up by the *Moors* Incursions, and those in *Misnia* and *Bohemia* not yet discover'd, all *Europe* was supplied with Tin from hence, to their great Advantage. The Benefit and Art of working Tin being now better discerned, the Gentlemen of *Cornwal,* in whose Grounds were many rich Mines, began to be sensible of the Gain they might make of it, and thereupon petition'd *Edmund,* Earl *Richard's* Son, to settle the Tinners under some better Rules, and grant them a Charter, which (upon an Agreement that they would pay the Earl an Halfpenny for every Pound of wrought Tin) was willingly yielded, and these Privileges by it settled upon them, (which now bear the Name of the *Stannary*-Laws) *viz.* That these Gentlemen should be authorized to keep a Court, which might hold Pleas for all Actions, (Life, Limb, and Land, only excepted) ; That for the bettering of the said Tax to the Earl, all the wrought Tin should be brought to certain Places appointed for that purpose, and there shall be weighed, coined and kept, until the said Tax was

satisfied ; That the said Gentlemen, for their Parts, should
have the Management of all Stannary-Causes, and to that
end might hold Parliaments at their Discretion, and in
respect to their Trouble, should be allowed a fifteenth
Man in all Tin-Mines within their Jurisdiction for Toll.
This Charter was confirmed with the Earl's own Seal, and
to be kept in one of the Steeples within the Tithings of the
said Gentlemen, who were Lords of them. This first
Charter was extant in the beginning of the last Century,
but is now lost. These Liberties, Privileges and Laws were
afterwards confirmed and enlarged by K. *Edward* III.
who divided the Body of Tinners into four Parts, denom-
inated from the Place where itis wrought, *viz. Foymore,
Blackmore, Tiwarnall,* and *Penrith.* He constituted one
general Warden or Overseer of all the rest, who is made
both in Causes of Law and Equity their supreme Judge,
from whom no Appeal lies but to the King and Council.
He hath Power to appoint under him a Sub-Warden over
every Company, who should every three Weeks, in their
respective Jurisdiction, determine all Controversies personal between the Tinners themselves or Foreigners, in
Matters relating to their Trade and Dealings ; but from
these an Appeal lies to the Lord Warden, before it can be
removed to the King. These are called Stannary-Courts
and Judgements. Their Manner of Trial ordinarily con-
sisteth in the Verdict of a Jury of six Tinners, according
to which the Warden or his Deputy pronounceth Judgment ; but in Matters of great Importance, the Lord or
his Deputy useth to impanel a Jury of 24 Men, principal
Tinners, six out of every Quarter, return'd by the Mayors
of the four Stannary Towns, and their Verdict obliges the
whole Body. [a] The Gaol for Offenders in Stannary Causes

---

a *This Privilege was granted the Tinners by a Charter given them by* is kept at *Lestwithiel,* and the Office is annexed to the Controllership, and the Pillory sometimes made their Punishment, as a Terror to others.

Having given this large Account of the Tin, we shall add something of the Mundick, which has of late begun to rival it in Value and Profit. It is a yellow Ore, mix'd with the Tin, a sulphureous Matter, of a sad brown, but glittering Colour. The Tinners thought it a sort of Earth which nourished the Tin, but of no Use when mixed with it, and therefore separated it from the Tin with great Care, because it made it thick and cruddy, it being ready enough to evaporate into a Smoak, which was very loathsome and stinking ; but of late it hath been try'd and wrought singly by some curious Undertakers, and is found to turn to a very great Advantage, by affording true Copper, which makes so good a Return, that the Tin-Trade it self is in danger of being neglected. This Mundick, as it is in some Respects very pernicious, *viz.* to the Miners, who are sometimes choaked with its unwholesome Steam, so in others 'tis very useful ; for being applied to a Wound, it immediately cures it, which the Workmen are so sure of, that they use no other Remedy than washing in the Water that runs from the Mundick-Ore ; but this must be done before it is wrought or burnt, for then the Water in which it is washed is so venomous, that it rancles Sores, and kills the Fish of any River it falls into ; yea, they say, some Men have been killed by drinking of such Water.

In speaking of the living Creatures, we shall begin

King Henry VII. *who having seiz'd the Stannaries into his own Hands, after his Son Prince* Arthur's *Death, because they would not observe his Constitutions, at length granted them a Pardon, upon their Payment of 1000l. for all Forfeitures, in which this Privilege was allowed them.*

with the Inhabitants, who are of brawny, stout, and able Bodies, which makes them delight in boisterous Exercises, as Wrestling, Hurling, *&c.* and enables them to carry prodigious Burdens, of which some Instances are given of a wonderful Nature ; as one *John Bray,* who carried on his Back six Bushels of Meal, 15 Gallons to the Bushel, and the Miller, a Man of 24 Years of Age, upon them ; one *John Roman,* a thick, short Fellow, who carried at one time the whole Carcass of an Ox ; and one *Kiltor,* who lying on his Back in *Launceston*-Castle, threw a Stone of some Pounds Weight to the top of the highest Tower of it. From this Strength of Body chiefly, tho' something may be imputed to the Goodness of the Air, it proceeds that many of the Inhabitants have prov'd very long-liv'd ; as one *Polzew* liv'd 130 Years, and a Kinsman of his 112 ; one *Beauchamp* 106, and one *Brown* 100, One Mr. *Chaumond* of *Stratton* was Uncle and Great Uncle to at least 300.

The Language of the *Cornish* Gentry and Yeomanry is *English,* and that as pure as is spoken at *London,* unless it be in two or three Parishes near the Land's-end, where the *Cornish* Language is most used.

Of tame Cattle, they have all the several Sorts that other Counties have, as Sheep, Cows, Horses, Swine, Dogs, *&c.* What is peculiar to this County is, the Sheep ; tho' when the Country lay open and waste, they were of little Bodies, and had so coarse Fleeces, that their Wool was called *Cornish* Hair ; yet since their Lands have been well manur'd and tilled, they now equal the Sheep of other Counties in Bigness of Body, and Fineness of Wooll, and excel them in Sweetness of Taste and Soundness of Flesh. They generally have no Horns, and they observe, that their Wooll is finer, tho' not so much as those that have ; yet in some Parts they have four Horns. Their Cows and Oxen are small, but their Flesh sweet ; and because they meet with good Markets often for victualling of Ships, (and sometimes they steal a Transportation) they are encouraged to rear great Numbers of Oxen for Beef. They use the Oxen also chiefly for Ploughing, which they manage so, that having given each Ox his Name, they can direct and encourage him in his Work by it, by calling them aloud.

Their Horses are hard-bred, coarsly fed, and quick in travel, tho' low of Stature ; which Sort is most serviceable for rough and hilly Countreys, as this is. They are naturally of a good Courage ; but by hard Labour in carrying Sand for Tillage when they are young, they are brought off their Metal, and become dull and sluggish. Moyls or Mules are much in use here, and that deservedly, for 'tis a Beast that will fare hard, live long, draw indifferently, will carry great Burdens, and go swiftly and easy.

As to wild Beasts, this County hath divers Parks stocked with fallow Deer ; but they have no red Deer, but what stray thither out of *Devon.* One thing is peculiar to this County, that some Gentlemen will suffer their Black Cattle to run wild in their Woods and waste Grounds, that they may have the Pleasure of hunting and killing them as Deer, whose Nature some of them seem to have put on. Many Otters, Badgers, Martens, and Foxes, also harbour in the Cliffs by the Sea-side ; rare Sport for the Gentlemen.

This County abounds with many Sorts of Fish, both in their Rivers and adjoining Bays of the Sea, as Trout,

Peal, Lobsters, Oysters, Soles, Flowks, Plaice, Brits, Smelts, Whitings, Sharks, Congers, Porpoises, and many others of lesser Note ; but the most advantageous Sort are Pilchards, the *Spanish* Capon, a small Fish which appears upon their Coasts in vast Swarms or Shoals from *July* to *November,* and are caught in such Quantities as are incredible. One Gentleman ('tis said) caught 500000 of them at one Draught, which, tho' unusual, yet is not exceeding Belief to such as see in what vast Shoals they appear, and with what Art they are taken. When they are thus catched, some of the Country-People, who attend with Horses and Panniers at the Cliff-side in great Numbers, buy them for their own Use, or to carry them up and down the Country, and sell to the more Inland Towns. The rest the Merchants, who make a great Trade of them, buy up, and fit them for foreign Markets three ways, by fuming, pressing, and pickling. For each of these, they are first garbag'd and salted, and piling them up in Heaps in some Cellar, let them lie ten Days, till the superfluous Moisture of the Blood and Salt is drained from them.

When this is done, they pack some up in Hogsheads with Pickle for *France,* but others without for hot Countreys, as *Spain* and *Italy.* They formerly dry'd them with the Smoke of a gentle Fire, from whence they were Called *Fumado's* ; but now they only put them on Sticks, and having washed them, pack them up close in Hogsheads with Leaks, and press them down with great Weights, that the Train may soak out, and so send them away, tho' they yet retain their old Name [a] abroad.

---

a *The* Spaniards *dress them with Oil and lime, and setting them before the Grandees, are accepted as a great Dainty.*

Multitudes of Sea-Fowl are seen upon these Coasts, as well as some Sorts by Land, *viz.* Gulls, Pewets, Sanderlings, Sea-pies, Larks, Oxen and Kine, Puffins, Curlews, Ducks and Mallards, Teal, wild Geese, and Barnacles, Choughs, Herons and Cranes, with many other kinds ; but of all these, they have the greatest Plenty of Woodcocks. The Eggs of divers of those Fowls are good to be eaten, and the young ones of others being taken as soon as they are feather'd, are made tame, fatted, and so fitted for the Table. The Barnacle is said to breed under Water, hanging by the Bill on the Sides of such Ships as have been long at Sea, till they become a perfect Bird ; but this is not clearly made out. The Puffin's young ones are very fat, and being salted up, are eaten for Fish, which they taste very like. I have before mentioned the *Cornish* Chough, the Disgrace of the Country for Mischief ; but 'tis only when he is kept tame, which makes it unlucky, because idle.

The Fruits and Herbs of this County are much the same with others, tho' not so plentiful among the common People. 'Tis thought that the nearness of it to the Sun gives it some Advantage for the planting and ripening Grapes, of which good Wines might be made for the Benefit of the People, especially where the Ground stands upon Lime-stones ; but no Trial has yet been made that way. Besides the common Herbs, this County has some either not found out at all, or not so plentifully in others, *viz.* small, creeping, round leav'd, bastard Chick-weed, wild Asparagus, round-leav'd Marsh St. *Peter's* Wort, tender Ivy, leav'd Bell-flower, the least Marsh Centaury, Fir-leav'd Heath with many Flowers, great yellow Marsh

Eye-bright, small Sea Cranes-bill, with Betony-Leaves, Sea Cud-weed or Cotton-weed, creeping Cocks's-foot Grass, smooth leav'd Rupture wort, the lesser Autumnal Star-Jacinth, and *English* Sea-Pease. They have also Plenty of Sea Herbs, as Samphire, Sea-holly, Eringo, *Ros Solis,* and Pelamontain with many fragrant Herbs, as Marjoram, Rosemary, *&c.* which grow wild upon the Cliffs.

The Waters of this County, tho' it is full of Mines, yet (which is very remarkable) are pleasant and wholesome, vary rarily tinged, or impregnated with any Mineral Taste, and every Province has one or more Springs of them. The Miners often find Springs crossing their Loads ; but Tin being of a close Body, and not apt to rust, the Waters that pass thro' them do nor partake at all of any Mineral Taste, or Medicinal Nature from it, as the Waters of *Epsom, Tunbridge, Dulwich, Streatham,* and many others do, which pass thro' Iron Mines. Yet this County does not altogether want Waters of a Physical Nature, as *Maddren's* Well near *Pensance,* whose Waters are so restorative, that they have cur'd some of their Lameness, others of the Cholick, and the like Distempers. *Scarlet's* Well also near *Bodmin,* tho' it was once superstitiously thought to cure all Diseases, which appear'd so gross an Error, that the Justices of Peace found it necessary to forbid all Resort to it ; yet it plainly seems to have an healthful Quality in it more than ordinary, because it is much weightier than other Water, will keep the best part of a Year without Alteration of Scent or Taste, and represents many Colours like the Rainbow. Here are no Purging-Waters, unless you will reckon *St. Kayn's* Well to purge Melancholy, the Nature of the Waters being vulgarly reported to be this:

The Person of that Man or Wife,
Whose Chance or Choice attains,

First of this sacred Stream to drink,
Thereby the Mastery gains.

The Islands of *Silly,* called in Latin *Silurum Insulæ,* and supposed to be the *Cassiterides* of the Ancients, have always been thought to belong to *Cornwal,* and therefore must be treated of here. They lie about 60 *Miles* from the Land's-End, and are in Number about 140. The chief of them is called *Silly,* and gives Name to all the rest ; but the Island of *St. Mary* is now the most fruitful and largest, yet is but three Leagues round. It has a very good Harbour, fortified by a Castle, which was built by Queen *Elizabeth.* It is very probable that they were heretofore joined to the main Land of *Cornwal,* and separated, by some violent Irruptions of the Sea, both from the Continent and from each other, because the Sea is much of the fame Depth, *viz.* between 40 and 60 Fathom quite over, unless about the Middle, where lies a Rock called St. *Michael's* Gulph, which, withstanding the Fury of the Water, makes a Prominency in the Bottom. These Isles were conquer'd by *Ethelstan,* one of the *Saxon* Kings of *England,* and from his Time have been subject to the Kings of *England,* and appertaining to this County. Ten of them are bigger than the rest, *viz. St. Mary, Silly, Annet, Agnes, Sampson, Byer, Tresco, St. Helena, St. Martin's,* and *Arthur's.* Some of them stand very high, but others are cover'd with Water at high Tide. Some of them bear good Corn, but most of them afford Pasture chiefly. They abound with Water-Fowl, as Cranes, Herons, Swans, &c. and have Plenty of Rabbets. The *Phœnicians, Carthaginians* and *Romans,* frequented the Tin-Mines here, and the latter sent their Criminals to dig in them ; but the Inhabitants now make very little of them, cementing themselves to live at Ease, and exchange small Parcels of Lead, Tin, and Skins, for Earthen and Brass Vessels and Salt. They have no Money, and live upon the Milk and Flesh of their Cattle, as the *Nomades* anciently did.

The Ecclesiastical History.

IT having been proved, beyond all Contradiction by our most learned Bishop of *Worcester,* Dr. *Stillingfleet,* that [a] the Christian Religion was planted in the Island of *Great Britain* in the Apostles Age, and that most probably by St. *Paul* ; and it appearing by our Histories, that the *Saxon* Invaders drove the *Britains* into the Western Parts of the Island beyond the *Severn* and *Cornwal,* when they possessed themselves of the other Parts of the Isle, and erected the Heptarchy, it must be recorded, for the eternal Honour of the *Cornish,* that they are some of the most ancient Christians of the Island, and tho' miserably harrass'd by the Heathen *Saxons,* kept up an Hierarchy and Royal Jurisdiction among themselves. We have no certain Account of their Dioceses, or Order of Government ; but we may collect from several Passages of the History of those Times, that *St. David's* was an Archbishop's See, and that there were six other Bishops his Suffragans, which the Latin calls, *Episcopi Herefordensis, Landavensis, Bangorensis, Paternensis, Elvensis,* and *Wicciorum,* three of which cannot now be fixed. This appears from the [b] Relation of the Conferences between the *British* Christians and St. *Austin,* at his first coming to convert the *Saxons.* Under which of these Bishops *Cornwal* was, we cannot determine, nor who were Bishops

---

a   Orig. Brit.
b   Bed. *lib.* 2. *c.* 2.

in the *British* Times, unless we will reckon (as Dr. *Heylin* does) St. *Petrocke* to be Bishop in *Cornwal* ; but be is so much mistaken in the Time, which he assigns to be *A. D.* 850, near 300 Years after his Death, as Dr. *Fuller* and Mr. *Collier* compute, that it is to be feared he mistakes also in the Office. But however that be, 'tis certain he was a very godly and zealous Preacher of the Gospel among the *Cornish,* and had his general Residence at the Town, now bearing his Name, *Patrock Stow, i.e.* St. *Patrock's* Place, but now called *Padstow* by Contraction. He had spent twenty Years in *Ireland,* in improving himself in the Study of Theology, for which that Nation, from the Days of St. *Patrick,* had been very famous, and having much edify'd the *Cornish* with his Doctrine, went into the *East Indies, i.e.* a far Country, from which he returned in his old Age, and living but a little time after, was buried at *Bodmin,* in the Church afterwards made a Cathedral, and dedicated to St. *Petrock.*

What was the State of the Churches, in the Kingdom of *Cornwal* after this, we read nothing of, till this County, by the Arms of King *Egbert* and *Athelstan,* became subject to the *Saxons.* Bishop *Godwin* seems to date the Conversion of *Cornwal* to the Christian Religion from this Time, and says, that it was subject to the Bishops of the *West-Saxons,* whose See was first at *Dorchester* near *Oxford,* then at *Winchester,* and at last *Shirburn* ; but it must be understood of the *Saxon* Christianity, which was that which was subject to the See of *Rome,* for the Apostolical they had received many Ages before ; nor is it credible that any thing but Force could have brought these *Britains* to submit to the Papal Jurisdiction, who had so resolutely opposed *Augustin* on that Account. King *Athelstan* then having subdued *Cornwal,* immediately order'd *Plegmund,* at that time Archbishop of *Canterbury,* to constitute them a Bishop, which he soon after did, having obtained Power of Pope *Formosus* to settle some new Sees in those Parts new conquer'd, *viz.* one at *Tawton* in *Devonshire,* (which had been subject to the Kings of *Cornwal*) and another at *Bodmin* in *Cornwal,* where was a Cathedral Church dedicated to St. *Petrock.* The first Bishop of this See was *Athelstan,* who had for his Successors, *Conan, Ruydocke, Aldred, Britwin, Athelstan* II., *Wolf, Woron, Wolocke, Stidie, Aldred,* and *Burwold* ; of all whom we find nothing memorable, but that in the Time of one of these last, the *Danish* Pyrates landing in *Cornwal,* burnt the Cathedral Church of St. *Petrock,* and the Bishop's Palace at *Bodmin,* which obliged the Bishop to remove to *St. Germans.* In the mean time, the Bishop's See at *Tawton* was removed to *Crediton* or *Kirton* in the same County, where *Sidmanus,* the 7th Bishop of that See, sat, when the Bishoprick of *Cornwal* was settled at *St. Germans,* about the Year 990. After him succeeded *Alfred, Alfwold, Eadnoth,* and *Levingus,* who being cotemporary with *Barwold,* Bishop of *St. Germans,* and outliving him, procured of *Canutus,* that his See should be united to *Crediton,* and so much the rather, because King *Etheldred* had much augmented the Revenue of *St. Germans.* He enjoy'd them both during his Life, which happen'd *A. D.* 1049 to have an end, and was succeeded by *Leofrick,* a *Burgundian,* nobly born, and singularly learned, who being a Privy Counsellor to King *Edward* the Confessor, obtained Leave of that King to remove his See from *Kirton* to *Exeter,* where it still remains.

The County of *Cornwal* shewing such Footsteps of Holiness, many Towns bearing the Name of a Saint, we must not be so uncharitable as to think that they were Imposed for any other Reason, but because they were born or lived here, and on that Account the People had such a Veneration for them, that they preserved their Memory that way. We shall mention some few, *viz.*

St. *Ursula*, the Daughter of *Dinoth* or *Deonotus*, Duke of *Cornwal*, who is said, with 11000 Virgins, to have sailed over into *Little Britain* or *Armorica* in *France*, there to be married to the *Britains*, their Countrymen, who refus'd to take them Wives from the *French* ; but being cast away in their Passage upon the *French* Shore they were murder'd by the Pagans, because they would not abandon their Religion and Chastity. Others say, they went to *Rome* to converse with Pope *Cyriacus*, and in their Return home were murder'd by King *Attila* the *Hunn* at *Colen*, where St. *Ursula* had a Church dedicated to her. We will not warrant this Story ; but 'tis sufficient for us if the first Part be true, let Papists believe the rest.

St. *Melorius*, the Son of *Melian* Duke of *Cornwal*, whom *Rinaldus*, his Pagan Brother, inhumanly butcher'd, cutting off first his Right Hand, then his Left Leg, and lastly his Head, about *A. D.* 411. His Relicks did many Miracles, which, in Gratitude, obliged the People to saint him.

St. *Keby*, Son to *Solomon* Duke of *Cornwal*, Scholar to St. *Hillary* of *Poictiers*, and a zealous Champion for the Purity of Religion against the Poison of *Arianism*. He was made a Bishop by St. *Hillary*, and settled himself in the Isle of *Anglesey*, where *Caer Guiby*, or *Holy-head* and *Hillary Point*, preserve the Names of the Master and

Scholar.

St. *Germanus,* who (with his holy Companion *Lupus*) suppressed the *Pelagian* Heresy, then much infesting this Isle. S. *Columba,* an exceeding pious Woman, and Martyr, St. *Buriana* or *Beriana,* a religious *Irish* Woman ; St. *Iia,* an *Irish* Woman of great Piety, with many others, which *Capgrave* recites in his Catalogue, and whose Names the *Cornish* Towns bear, we can only mention, because they were such *British* Saints as had deny'd Subjection to *Augustin, the Saxon* Apostle, Archbishop of *Canterbury),* and so they are marked by the *Saxon* Historians rather as Hereticks than Saints ; for the Record in *Spelman* [a] says, They were Enemies to the Truth and the Pope's Authority ; much such a Reason as the *Jews* had for branding St. *Paul* with that Name.

We come now to the Religious Houses in this County, which were not many, nor very considerable. The *Britains* were much addicted to this sort of holy Living, as may appear from that eminent Monastery of *Bangor,* wherein were above two thousand Monks ; but we do not find that there were any Monasteries erected in *Cornwal,* till it became subject to the *Saxons,* under the Government of King *Athelstan,* by whom

St. Germans, a Monastery of Canons Regular of St. *Augustin,* was erected ; but it was found by an Inquisition in the 30th Year of K. *Edward* III. that K. *Canute* endowed this Church, and that it was then a Bishop's Seat for *Cornwal,* and College of Canons Secular ; but when the Bishops were removed to *Crediton,* and then to

---

a Con. *Vol.* I. *p.* 387.

Exeter, Leofricus, the first Bishop of *Exeter,* turned it into a Priory of Canons Regular, of which he made the Bishops of *Exeter* for the Time being perpetual Patrons, who had the Privilege of enjoying the Profits of all Vacations in the said Priory. The Value of the Revenues of this Abbey at the Suppression was *243l.* 8*s.* 9*d.* as both *Dugdale* and Mr. *Speed* agree.

Bodmin, an Abbey of *Benedictine* Monks, was also founded by K. *Athelstan.* Mr. *Tanner* says, 'twas at *Petrockstow* or *Padstow* by Mistake ; for the Monasticon settles this Abbey at *Bodmin* : *S. Petrocus Monasticam professus Vitum est sub Regula Benedicti apud Bedeminiam,* &c. This Monastery, dedicated to St. *Petrock,* was destroyed by the *Danish* Pyrates *A. D.* 981, and not rebuilt till 1110, at which Time Earl *Algar,* with the Consent of Bishop *Warlewast,* restor'd it, and put in black Canons, the Revenues in the mean time being appropriated to his own Use by the Earl of *Moriton* and *Cornwal. Leland* tells us, That this Monastery suffer'd many Changes, for the Monks settled by *Algar* were forced to give Place to Nuns, and they again to Secular Priests, whom the Monks within a while dispossessed, yet were again constrained co make room for Canons Regular. We find no more of this Monastery but this, that King *Henry* III. in the 57th Year of his Reign, confirmed to the Prior and Canons of *Bodmin* the Manor of *Newton* in *Devon,* formerly given them by King *Eadred,* with an Exemption from Suit to the County of *Devon* and Hundred of *Shesbury,* &c. Valued at *270l.* 11*d. per Annum* by *Dugdale,* and 289*l.* 11*s.* 11*d.* by *Speed.*

St. Buriens, a College of Secular Canons, founded by the same King *Athelstan.* It consisted of a Dean and three Prebendaries in the 20th Year of King *Edward* I. This Deanery is probably still in being, and subordinate to the See of *Exeter* ; for we find Dr. *Creighton,* Dean of *Burians,* made Dean, and after Bishop of *Wells,* in the Reign of King *Charles* II. Value not found. *Speed* seems to call it *Bonnry.*

Launceston, a Collegiate Church, built for Canons Regular of St. *Augustin* before the Conquest, and dedicated to St. *Stephen.* It stood in the Suburbs of this Town, in the South-West Part, but was suppressed by Bishop *Warlewast,* who put in *Augustin* Friars into their Places, and giving the greatest Part of the Lands to the Priory, kept the rest for himself. *Reginald* Earl of *Cornwal* was a great Benefactor to this House, 16th of King *Stephen,* A. D. 1150, and King *John* and King *Henry* III. confirmed the Lands given them by all their Benefactors. Valued, 26 *Henry* VIII. at 354*l.* 11*d. Dugd.* but 392*l.* 11*s.* 2*d. Speed.*

St. Michael's-Mount, an Abbey of *Benedictines,* founded by *Edward* the Confessor. *Robert* Earl of *Moriton* and *Cornwal* annexed it to God and the Church of *St. Michael de Periculo Maris* in *Normandy* about the Year 1085. *Richard* King of the *Romans, Edmund* Earl of *Cornwal,* and *Conan* Duke of *Britany,* were Benefactors to this House, and Pope *Adrian,* in the Year 1155, confirmed to the Abbot and Monks of this House, By the Name of the Monastery of *St. Michael de Periculo Maris,* all their Lands and Revenues, lying most in *Normandy,* but many in *England.* After the Suppression of Priories alien, it was given to *Sion* College near *Brentford* in *Middlesex.*

Trueardaith, or (as the Monasticon has it) *Tywer-*

dreit, a *Benedictine* Monastery, built up on the Bay so called, which is now increas'd to a Village. It was founded by *Robert de Cardinan* in the Reign of King *Richard* I. and dedicated to St. *Andrew.* He gave divers Lands and Revenues to it, and annexed it as a Cell to S. *Sergius* and S. *Bachus* at *Angiers.* King *Henry* III. confirmed his and all other Grants to the Monks of it. It survived the Suppression of the Alien Priories, but fell at the general Dissolution, when it was found to be endowed with Lands and other Revenues to the Value us 123*l.* 9*s.* 3*d. Dngdale.* 151*l.* 16*s.* 1*d. Speed.*

Glasseney in *Perin,* a Collegiate Church, founded by *Walter Bronscomb,* the Bishop of *Exeter,* for one Dean, thirteen Canons, and as many Vicars, about the Year 1275. He is said to have been warned in a Vision or Dream to build it. He dedicated it to the Blessed Virgin *Mary* and St. *Thomas* of *Canterbury. Peter Quivil,* Bishop of *Exeter,* in the Year 1288, made a farther Provision for the Vicars, and Bishop *Grandison,* his Successor in the same See, was a liberal Benefactor to it. The great Ruins still remaining, are a plain Evidence that it was a very noble and costly Structure. The Endowments of it at the Suppression were valued at 205*l.* 10*s.* 6*d. Dugdale* and *Speed.*

St. Anthony, a Cell for two Canons only, annexed to *Plimpton* Priory. It is probable the Town arose from it, and still retains the Name, tho' there are no Signs of the House.

Helston, a small Priory, dedicated to S. *John Baptist,* which, at the Dissolution, was found to be in Value 12*l.* 16*s.* 4*d. Dugd.* 14*l.* 7*s.* 4*d. Speed.*

St. Syriac or *St. Caricius,* was a Cell to *Montacute* in

Somersetshire. It was a House for Black Monks, and bore the Name of the Saint to whom it was dedicated.

Crantocke, a College, valued at 89*l.* 15*s.* 8*d. Speed.*

Talearn, a Monastery for Black Monks of the Angels, (as Mr. *Speed* terms them and three other Monasteries in this County.) Mr. *Tanner,* a Person well skilled in these Matters, declares himself ignorant who these Monks of the Angels were, and therefore, if they were not such as pretended to more exalted and angelical Purity and Meditations than other Orders, we must leave it to the most Learned and Judicious to find out.

St. Mary Wyke, a Chantry, with a Free-School, erected and endowed by *Thomasine Bonaventure,* who from a poor Girl became after two other Husbands, wealthy Citizens, the Wife to Sir *John Percival,* Lord Mayor of *London,* whom also out-living, she employed her Widowhood in Works of Piety and Charity, as repairing High-ways, building Bridges, portioning poor Maidens, relieving Prisoners, and feeding the Indigent ; and among other Things, founded this Chantry and Free-School, with fair Lodgings for the Schoolmasters, Scholars, and Officers, and 20*l.* a Year for incident Charges ; a beneficial Charity, which Rich as well as Poor were the better for, because of the good Education of their Children there ; but the Chantry ruin'd the School ; for the Suppression of the one by the Statute *Edw.* VI. involved the other.

Roche, an huge, high, and steep Rock, the Habitation of an Hermit, who dwelt on the top of it, to whom the uneasy climbing up to his Cell and Chapel, which was part of it, carved out of the Rock, was Merit sufficient to entitle him to the Name of a Saint.

There are some other Religions Houses, whose Names are preserved to us, which may not be improper to mention, that the Diligent and Inquisitive may make farther Discoveries of them, as *Sante Cruz* for Black Monks, *St. Mary de Val* for Black Monks of the Angels, *St. Michael de Magno-Monte* for Black Monks, *Sully* Island for the same, and *Trury* for *Dominicans,* which, since the Learned can give no farther Account of, must be left to Posterity to search into.

It may not be amiss here to observe, that among the Multitudes of Martyrs that suffer'd for the Truth in King *Henry* VIII's Reign, and Queen *Mary's* we find no *Cornish* Man or Woman, which is taken Notice of by the Martyrologist himself, who gives us this good Reason, that they were at such a Distance from *London,* that their Faith did not come upon Examination ; so happy a thing it is for good Men to be out of Harm's way.

Learned DIVINES *who either lived or were born in this County.*

JOhn of *Cornwal,* a Student at *Rome,* and other Universities in *Italy,* who wrote about the Incarnation of Christ against *Peter Lombard,* and dedicated it to Pope *Alexander* III. by whom he was highly favour'd.

William de Grenefeld, Archbishop of *York* in the Reign of *Edward I.* was born in this County : (He was also Chancellor of *England* at the same time) As were also

Michael Tregury, Archbishop of *Dublin* in K. *Henry* VI's Reign, [a] and

John Arundel, Bishop of *Coventry* and *Lichfield* in K. *Henry* VII's Time : And if we may have Leave to mention the Living among the Dead, 'tis no small Honour to this County, that

Sir *Jonathan Trelawney,* the present Bishop of *Winchester,* is a Native of it.

After these worthy Prelates, we may pass to other Divines eminent in their Generation, *viz.*

Simon Thurnay, who having obtained to a great Eminency in Learning at *Oxford,* went and study'd Divinity at *Paris,* and became one of the most celebrated Doctors of the *Sorbonne.*

Godfrey de Cornwal, a very cunning Schoolman, and Divinity-Reader at *Paris.* Dr. *Baconthorp,* his Cotemporary, calls him Dr. *Solennis, i.e.* The grave Doctor. He flourish'd about the Year 1310.

John Trevisa, who lived in the Reign of K. *Richard* II. was one of the Translators of the Bible ; and tho' he was inclin'd to *Wickliff's* Doctrine, yet lived to a great Age without any Disturbance. He died in the Reign of the said King.

---

a *He was so famous for his Learning and Gravity before he was raised to this exalted Dignity, that King* Henry V. *having founded an University at* Caen *in* Normandy, *appointed him to be the Governor or Rector of it, from whence King* Henry VI. *removed him to the See of* York.

Thomas Vivian, Suffragan Bishop to the Bishop of *Exeter,* under the Title of *Episcopus Magarenses.* He was also Rector of *Exeter* College, *Oxford.*

Bartholomew Traharon, Library-Keeper to K. *Edward* VI. and Dean of *Chichester.*

Charles Herle, Prolocutor of the Assembly of Divines, and Rector of *Winnick* in *Lancashire,* the greatest Parsonage in *England.*

The CHARITY-SCHOOLS *of this County are at*

ST. Colomb, where are twelve Boys and eight Girls taught and cloathed.

Grampound, where there is a School endowed with 20*l.* a Year by a private Gentleman, who has also settled an Annuity of 100*l.* a Year, for Ninety nine Years, towards the Support of this and four other Charity-Schools at

Leskard,	*Pensance,* and
Looe,	*Saltash.*

Launceston, where are two Schools for forty eight Children of both Sexes. The Boys are taught to read and write, and the Girls to knit, sew, and make Bone-lace, and they are to have their Earning for Encouragement.

Morvell, where a Gentleman has given a House and Garden, with 8*l.* a Year, to teach poor Children for ever.

Polperra, near *Looe,* where is a School for teaching as many poor Girls as the Interest of 100*l.* will pay. It was a Legacy left for that purpose.

An Account of the Boroughs in Cornwal ; Extracted from several Authors and Accounts sent.

THIS County abounds with Parliamentary Boroughs or Corporations ; for besides the Towns that at present send Members to Parliament, there are these following Corporations, *viz. Falmouth, Market-Jew, Pensance* and *Padstow, Botereux Castle, Crofthole, Milbrooke,* and *Stratton,* which never sent Members to Parliament, nor ever were summoned otherwise ; not above six or seven Boroughs had that Privilege before the Reign of K. *Edward* VI. and Qu. *Elizabeth.* It is supposed that they were so made by the Interest of their Earls.

When the Parliament was summoned to sit at what Places the King thought fit, which were often changed, the Knights and Burgesses of this County were allowed for their going to and coming from *Cambridge,* six Days ; *Coventry,* eight ; *York,* eleven or twelve ; *Gloucester,* four or five ; *Leicester,* six ; *Lincoln,* nine ; *London* and *Westminster,* seven or eight ; *Northampton,* six, and in bad Weather, ten ; *Nottingham,* seven and a half ; *Salisbury,* three ; and *Winchester,* five.

The Catalogue of the Knights who served in Parliament for this Shire begins the 23d of *Edward* I. but is imperfect ; the Writs, Indentures and Returns, from the 17th of K. *Edward* IV. to the first of K. *Edward* VI. being lost throughout *England,* except one imperfect Bundle ; but from thence continued down to the 12th of Queen *Anne.* The Members for the present Parliament are,

John Trevanion Esq; and

Sir *William Carew* Bar.

1.   *Borough of* Dunhivid *alias* Launceston.

IT is called *Dunhivid* from its Situation, being built on the Top or Head of a Down or Hill ; and *Launceston,* contracted from *Lanstaphadon, i.e.* The Church of St. *Stephen.* It was built by *Eadulfus,* Brother of *Alpsius* Duke of *Devon* and *Cornwal. William* the Conqueror gave it *Robert* Earl of *Morton* and *Cornwal,* his Half-Brother, and by *Richard* Earl of *Poictiers* and *Cornwal,* Brother of King *Henry* III. it was made a free Borough, having Liberty granted the Burgesses to chuse their own Bailiffs, and erect a Guild or Fraternity of Merchants to hold of him and his Heirs. These Privileges were confirmed often afterwards, and other Liberties added, *viz.* That the Assizes and Sessions should be kept no where else, *Anne* to *Richard* II. *&c.* The Manor of this Town hath been invested upon the eldest Sons of the Kings of *England* ever since K. *Richard* II. as it now continues.

The free Burgesses and Mayor, who are in Number 130, elect the Members for Parliament. It was incorporated by Queen *Mary, Anno* 1555. It is an ancient Market-Town, and the Market in K. *John's* Days was kept on *Sundays* ; but for a Fine of five Marks, was alter'd to *Thursday,* and since is removed to *Saturdays,* as it now remains.

Leland tells us, *Itin.* Vol. VII. that in his Time it was walled in, and a Mile in Compass ; that it, had a Castle standing in the N.W. Side of it ; and that some Gentlemen held their Lands by Castle-guard, *i.e.* To repair and defend the Castle ; and that at a little Distance from the Castle Northward was a Priory of Canons Regular, dedicated to St. *Stephen.* The present Parish-Church was made out of a Chantery-Chapel, enlarged in the Time of *Henry* IV. and made big enough to receive the Inhabitants of the Town. 'Tis graced with an handsome high Tower, and a beautiful Statue of St. *Mary Magdalen,* to whom it is dedicated.

The List of the Burgesses for this Town begins the 23d of *Edward I.* and is continued (with the same Defect as in the County) to the 12th Year of Queen *Anne.* The present Burgesses are,

> *John Anstis* Esq; and
> *Edward Hearle* Esq;

2. *Borough of* Leskard.

WAS given likewise by *William* the Conqueror to *Robert* Earl of *Morton* and *Cornwal,* and made a free Borough by *Richard* Earl of *Poictiers* and *Cornwal,* who procured the Burgesses here the same Privileges as had been before granted to *Launceston* and *Helston,* which he settled on them by a Charter, bearing Date *June* 5, 1240. His Son *Edmund* granted this Borough, with all the Tolls and Rents, to the Townsmen in Fee-farm, at the Rent of 18*l. per Annum,* which they have held ever since, and paid to the Dutchy, till the late King *William* III. bestowed it on the Lord *Somers,* to whom they are now paid by the Corporation.

This Town was incorporated by Queen *Elizabeth July 6,* 1580, who appointed a Mayor and Burgesses, and order'd that they should have a perpetual Succession, purchase Lands, *&c.* The Election of their Members for Parliament is vested in the nine Capital Burgesses, of whom one is always a Mayor, and their fifteen Assistants, with other Freemen, who are now in Number about a hundred.

It is a large and populous Town, containing about 100 Houses. The Market is one of the most considerable in the County, and the Buildings handsome. The Church is a large Fabrick, with a broad Tower, dedicated to St. *Martin,* and is well pav'd. The Patronage of the Church anciently belonged to the Priory of *Launceston,* to which the great Tithes were appropriated, and at the Dissolution was granted to one Mr. *Connock,* to whose Descendants it still belongs.

Here was anciently a Castle on the North Side, with a Park, and Chapel of our Lady, famous for the many Pilgrimages made to it adjoining ; of which now little or nothing remains but the Site. In the Town is an admirable Conduit, which plentifully supplies the Streets about the Market-place with Water. This is one of the Towns for Coinage of Tin, and is remarkable for the Defeat of the Parliament-Army *Anno* 1642 by Sir *Ralph Hopton,* of which there is yet a Memorial kept in the Church. The Market in *Leland's* Time was kept on the *Monday* Weekly, but is now on *Saturday.* On the Top of the Town-Hall, which is a goodly Building, there is a noble Clock, with four Dials, which cost near 200*l.* erected by Mr. *Dolben,* one of their Members for Parliament.

The Corporation hath two large Maces well gilt, and several Cups of Silver gilt, round one of which, in most constant Use, is engraved this Motto, *Qui fallit Poculum, fallit in omnibus* ; with other Plate, most of it Presents made them by Members of their Body.

The List of their Parliament-men begins the 23d of *Edward* I. and is continued entire (excepting the fore-mentioned Defect) to the 12th Year of Queen *Anne.* The present Members are,

> *John Trelawney* Esq; and
> *Philip Rashleigh* Esq;

3.   *Borough of* Lestwwithiel.

IS thought to have been the *Uzella* of *Ptolomy,* and anciently to have stood on an Hill, where the old Castle *Lestormel* shews its Ruins. The publick Buildings are long since defaced, and nothing remains of them but a small Part, repaired for a Prison and Stannary Court, which is kept there for Coinage of Tin. It is an ancient Corporation, belonging to the Dutchy, made by *Richard* Earl of *Cornwal* when he was King of the *Romans,* by a Charter dated at *Watlington. Penknek,* a Place adjoining, now a Part of it, had the same Privileges confered on it by the same Charter.

The Representatives of this Place for Parliament are chosen by the seven Burgesses, and their 17 Assistants. 'Tis a poor Place, yet holds the Anchorage in the Harbour, and Bushelage of Coals, Salt, Corn, *&c.* in the Town of *Fowey,* a Port a little lower on the River. The Buildings are mean, the Church dedicated to St. *Bartholomew,* not unsuitable, yet has a Spire-Steeple, which none else has in this County. It was abominably prophaned by the Parliament Soldiers in 1644, who also defaced several stately Buildings, as the great Hall and Exchequer of the Dukes of *Cornwal,* who had their Palace here. It was anciently the Shire-Town, and still the Knights of the Shire are chosen here, and the County Weights and Measures are kept here, by the Assignment of the Act of Parliament *Anno* 11 *Henry* VII.

It is probable *William* the Conqueror gave it to *Robert* Earl of *Morton* ; but being bestowed afterwards on *Richard* King of the *Romans,* with the former Towns, became part of the Dutchy of *Cornwal,* of which it still holds, paying 11*l.* 19*s.* 10*d. per Ann.* for their Liberties. It hath returned Members to Parliament ever since the 33d of King *Edward* I. and so has continued, as appears by the List, (excepting the former Defect) to the Death of Queen *Anne.* The present Representatives are,

_ _ _ _ *Liddel* Esq; and

Horatio Walpole Esq;

4.　*Borough of* Truro.

IT is called *Truergeu* in *Domesday*-Book, and was given by K. *William* the Conqueror to the aforesaid *Robert* Earl of *Cornwal* and *Morton*. *Richard Lucy* becoming Lord of this Town, procur'd it the Privilege of Soc, Toll, Them, and Ingfangthef, and not to plead or be impleaded in the Hundred or County-Courts, *&c.* It had a Market and Fair *Anno* 30 *Edward* I. when it was the possession of *Thomas de Prydias*, who maintained its Privileges, and held the Bailiwick of *Powdrishire* in Fee.

It afterwards became Part of the Demesnes of the Crown, tho' by what Means is not known ; for K. *Edw.* II. *Anno Reg.* 12. 1472, granted this Honour, Borough, Manor, and Hundred, to his Brother *George* Duke of *Clarence.* In *Leland's* Time it had a Castle, which stood a quarter of a Mile on the West Side of *Truro,* and belonged of old to the Dukes of *Cornwal,* but was then entirely demolished. It had a Monastery for White Friars standing in *Kenwen-street.* The Church, which is dedicated to the Virgin *Mary,* is a large Fabrick, built part of Moor-stone in an antique Form, and part of Stone of another kind. It hath a Nave Tower, one Isle, and part of another, which is left unfinished.

This Town was incorporated by *Reginald Fitz-Roy,* natural Son to K. *Henry* I. by the Name of a Mayor and Burgesses, who have large Privileges enjoyed by Prescription, *viz,* to be Mayor of *Falmouth,* and take the Keyage of the Goods laden and unladen there. It is a fair, large, and well traded Town, and has the Benefit of Coinage of Tin. It has two Markets weekly, well frequented, and not inferior to any Place in the County for Buildings. The Increase of *Falmouth* has something lessen'd the Number of Inhabitants here ; but still it is populous. It gives the Title of Baron to the Rt. Hon. the Earl of *Radnor.* The List of its Members sent to Parliament begins the 23d of K. *Edward* I. and is continued to the Death of Qu. *Anne,* but with the fore-mention'd Chasm. The present Members for this Borough are,

Colonel *Selwin,* and

Spencer Cowper Esq;

5.   *Borough of* Bodmin.

OWes its Rise to St. *Petroc,* who being translated hither from *Petrockstown* or *Padstow,* where he died and was buried, a famous Church was built here in Honour to him, which afterwards, in the Reign of K. *Edward* the Elder, became an Episcopal See, *A. C.* 926. but the *Danish* Pirates destroy'd it *A. C.* 981.

William the Conqueror found the Abbey in this desolate Condition, and bestow'd the Possessions of it upon his Brother *Robert* Earl of *Morton* and *Cornwal,* who taking them from those who had unjustly seiz'd them, converted them to his own Use during his Life ; but after his Death, *Algar* Duke of *Cornwal,* with the Assistance of *William Warlewast* Bishop of *Exeter,* re-edified it *A. D.* 1110, and placed Black Canons in it, who continued there till the Dissolution, when it was valued at 270*l.* 11*s.*

Dugd, but 289*l.* 11*s.* 11*d. Speed.* The Manor and Royalty, in which was a Market, Fair, and 68 Houses, with the Privilege of Gallows, Pillory, and View of Frank-pledge, was held by this Church ; but was leased out to the Burgesses to farm at a certain Rent to them, and 15*l. per Ann.* to a School, which the King augmented with 5*l. per Annum* more.

This Town was anciently governed by a Mayor and 36 Burgesses, which are now changed into a Mayor, 12 Aldermen, 24 Common-Council Men, and a Town Clerk. The Members of Parliament are chosen by the Majority of the Corporation, and the Manor belongs to the Earl of *Radnor.* It had anciently several Churches and Chapels, of which nothing remains but Ruins, except one that formerly belonged to the Priory, which is now made the Parish-Church. Here was also a House for Grey-Friars on the South Part of the Town, a Chapel and Alms-house, but not endowed, and an Hospital dedicated to St. *Lawrence,* and founded for 19 Lazars, two whole Men and Women, a Priest to minister to them in a Chapel adjoining, and a Chantery, called St. *John Baptist*'s or *Naylor's* Chantery, founded in the Parish-Church by one *Naylor,* who gave a Revenue of 6*l. per Ann.* for one Priest to celebrate there for ever. He was a Chancery-Clerk, and Native of this Town.

The List of the Representatives of this Place begins the 23d of King *Edward* I. and is continued (except the former Defect) down to the 12th of Queen *Anne.* The present Members for this Corporation are,

The Hon. *Francis Roberts* Esq; and

_ _ _ _ *Leigh* Esq;

6.   *Borough of* Helston.

I S the King's Demesne still, as it is called in *Domesday*-Book, and is held of the Kings of *England* by the Townsmen, under a certain Quit-Rent of 13*l.* 6*s.* 8*d.* which they pay for the Toll, Mills, and 33 Acres of Land adjoining, to hold in Fee-farm, according to a Charter granted them by King *John, 2 Reg. A. D.* 1200, of whom they purchased for a Fine of 40 Marks, and one Palfrey, the Liberty to build them a Merchants-Guild, to pay no Toll but in the City of *London,* to be impleaded no where but in their own Borough, and to enjoy the Privileges of the Burgesses of *Launceston*-Castle.

King *Edward* III. farther granted them, at their Petition, a *Saturday* Market, and four Fairs yearly, *viz.* on the Eve, Day and Morrow, 1. of St. *Simon* and *Jude* ; 2. Of *Palm-Sunday* ; 3. Of St. *Cyricus* and *Julitta, July* 9, and of the Decollation of St. *John Baptist.*

This Town, tho' an ancient Borough, was not incorporated till the 27th of Queen *Elizabeth,* who appointed a Mayor and four Aldermen, who are to be of the Common-Council, and chuse 24 Assistants ; which Charter being confirmed by K. *Charles* I. he granted, That the Mayor for the Time being, Recorder, and preceding Mayor, should be always Justices of the Peace within the Borough, and keep a Quarter-Sessions.

The Members for Parliament for this Town are always elected by the sworn Freemen of the Corporation, who are about 70 Inhabitants, and 10 Out-Burgesses or Freemen. The Manor belongs to the Dukes of *Cornwal.* The Town is built in the Form of a Cross, and hath a large Market-House in the Centre of it, and a Guild-Hall at the Northern End. It is one of the four Stannary or Coinage-Towns and has four Streets, every one of which is well supplied with Water, because it has a little Chanel running thro' it. The Church, which is annexed to the Vicaridge of *Guendron,* is a large Building, and dedicated to St. *Michael,* on which Saint's Day the Mayor is chosen. The Steeple is 90 Foot high, and a Sea-Mark ; the Church 126 Foot long, and 41 broad, and kept in good Repair, the Town having no Dissenters in it. It had formerly a Castle, and a Priory or Hospital, dedicated to St. *John Baptist,* standing at the West End of the Town, which at the Dissolution was valued at 12*l.* 16*s. Dugd.* 14*l.* 7*s.* 4*d. Speed.* The Inhabitants at the Poll-Tax in 1694 were 1348, and their Number is since increased.

The List of such Members as have served in Parliament for this Borough begins the 23d of K. *Edward* I. and is continued (except the former Defect) to the 12th of Qu. *Anne.* The present Representatives are,

Sir *Gilbert Heathcote* Kt. and

Sidney Godolphin Esq;

7.   *Borough of* Saltash.

FOrmerly called *Essa,* stands on the Sea-Shore on the Side of a Hill, and contains near 200 Families. It belongs to the Honour of *Trematon Castle,* from which it derives several large Privileges over the Haven belonging to it, *viz.* a yearly Rent for all Boats and Barges, Anchorage of Shipping, and dragging of Oysters, except between *Candlemas* and *Easter.* It stands in the Parish of St. *Stephen,* to which it is a Chapel of Ease, dedicated to St. *Nicholas,* and is a decent Building, containing a Body, South-Ile, and Tower 57 Foot and a half high.

It has a Weekly Market kept on *Saturdays,* and a Claim to another on *Tuesdays,* but not observed, and two Fairs upon *July* 25, and *February* 2, yearly. The Manor of this Borough is vested in the Corporation, who hold it of the Dutchy of *Cornwal* ; and upon the Payment of a Fee-farm Rent of 18*l. per Ann.* have all the Toll of the Market and Fairs, K. *William* III. bestowed the Rents of all the Dutchy of *Cornwal* upon the Lord *Somers,* to whom they are now paid ; but out of that of this Town, 7*l. per Ann.* is paid to the Free-School, by an Endowment from the Crown.

Near the Chapel stands the Market-House and Town-Hall, which is an handsome Building, and the said School. The Corporation, by the Charter now in force, which was obtained 35 *Car.* II. 1682, consists of a Mayor, six Aldermen, and about 20 Freemen or Burgesses, who have Liberty to chuse them a Recorder, elect the Members of Parliament, which it first sent in K. *Edward* IV.'s Days, tho' it was made a Borough by *Reginald de Valletort,* Lord of the Honour of *Trematon* in K. *Henry* IV's Days, from whom, Male Issue failing, it was sold to *Richard* Earl of *Cornwal,* K. *Henry* III's Brother ; after whose Death it became vested in the Crown.

K. *Edward* III. settled this Town, part of the Manor of *Trematon,* and Park thereunto belonging, upon the

Black Prince and his Heirs, Dukes of *Cornwal,* and eldest Sons of the Kings of *England,* and granted the Advowson of the Church of St. *Stephen,* with the Tithes of *Saltash,* to his Collegiate Church of *Windsor,* by a Charter dated *May* 2, 1351.

The List of the Representatives for this Borough begins the 6th of K. *Edward* VI. and is continued to the 12th of Qu. *Anne.* The present Members are,

Shilston Calmady Esq; and
William Shippen Esq;

8.　　*Borough of* Camelford.

IS a mean Town, of not above 50 or 60 Houses, but an ancient Borough, created by *Richard* Earl of *Cornwal,* who, when he was King of the *Romans,* by his Charter granted the Burgesses of it a *Friday*-Market, and a Fair on the Eve, Day and Morrow of St. *Swithin,* which were all of them confirmed by his Brother K. *Henry* III. by his Charter dated *June* 12, 1259.

This Borough began to send Burgesses to Parliament in the Reign of K. *Edward* VI. and was throughly authoriz'd to continue it by Qu. *Mary,* who confirm'd their Liberties. It is at present govern'd by a Mayor and eight Burgesses or Aldermen, who, with 10 Freemen, elect their Members for Parliament. The Corporation enjoys the Toll of the Markers and Fairs, with an Estate of 15*l.* *per Annum,* which making together a Revenue of about 80*l. per Annum,* serve for the Support of, otherwise, a very mean Magistracy.

This Town is but an Hamlet to the Parish of *Lante-glos,* to the Church of which Place, distant about a Mile, the Inhabitants repair for the Worship of God, having never had (so far as we can learn) any Chapel at *Camelford.* The Manor is held of the Dutchy of *Cornwal,* as that of the former Towns.

This Town is famous for two remarkable Battels, the one fought between King *Arthur* and his Nephew *Mordred,* who being mortally wounded, was convey'd to *Glastenbury,* and there died, *May* 22, 542, the other between the *Britains* and *Saxons, A. D.* 823.

The List of Parliament-men for this Town begins the 6th of *Edward* VI. and is continued to the 12th of Qu. *Anne.* The present Members are,

James Montague Esq; and
Richard Coffen Esq;

9. *Borough of* Port-Pigham *alias* Westlow.

CAn't boast of any Antiquity, because it has no Par-ish-Church, which (says *Leland)* is a certain Sign that it is a new Town, sprung from a small Hamlet. It consists of about 100 Houses, and had formerly by Charter a *Wednesday* Market, and a Fair for three Days ; but this last is kept only one Day at present, *viz. April* 25. 'Tis in the Parish of *Talland,* a small Town a Mile distant, where the Inhabitants go to Church, and bury their Dead, for in this Village there is not so much as a Chapel remaining. We find that there was one in the Time of King *Henry* VIII. but being desecrated at the Dissolution of the Chanteries, was probably turned into the Guild-Hall of the Borough, as Tradition reports, and the Tower not long since standing by it may prove.

It was incorporated by Qu. *Elizabeth February* 14, 1574, by the Name of a Mayor and Burgesses, which latter were allowed to be twelve, and the Mayor to be annually chosen out of them, who together had Power to chuse a Steward, and have a Common-Seal. The Election of Members of Parliament is to be made by the said Corporation and the other Freemen, being about 60 in Number. In the first Return of Burgesses to serve in Parliament, 'tis called in the Indenture *Loubourough,* and in some others *Port-pigham, Portloo,* and *Westloo.*

The Lords of the Manor were first of the Family of *Treverbin,* who originally incorporated it, and made it a Borough : From them it descended to the *Carminows* and *Courtneys,* and at length was united to the Dutchy by King *Henry* VIII. in lieu of the Honour of *Wallingford* and St. *Waleyes,* which he had separated from it. The Rents of the Manor were then valued at 55*l.* and the Fee-farm at *Portloo* at 15*l.* 6*s.* 10*d.*

The List of Burgesses for this Borough begins the 6th of K. *Edward* VI. and is continued to the 12th of Qu. *Anne.* The present Members are,

George Delaval Esq; and
Thomas Maynard Esq;

10. *Borough of* Grampound.

IS a Town of no great Antiquity, and but meanly filled with Inhabitants. It was once a Market-Town ; but the Market is now near lost. It has but one Street of about 80 Houses, and lies in the Parish of *Creed,* yet has a small ordinary Chapel, dedicated to St. *Naunter* or St. *Nunn,* a Daughter of a certain Earl of *Cornwal,* and Mother to St. *David,* Archbishop of that See, (her Name being written in some Accounts *Nannita, Novita, Nunnites)* which is still in Use for the Service of God.

It is a Town Corporate, and has a Mayor, eight Magistrates, a Recorder, and Town-Clerk. The Mayor is annually chosen the *Tuesday* before *Michaelmas*-Day, and the Representatives for the Parliament by the Majority of the Magistrates and Freemen, who are all the Inhabitants that pay Scot and Lot, being about 50 in Number. It was made a Borough in the Time of King *Edward* III. but did not send Burgesses to Parliament till the Reign of K. *Edward* VI.

'Tis an ancient Manor belonging to the Dutchy, endowed with large Privileges by K. *Edward* III's Charter, *viz.* with several Lands and Mills, View of Frank-pledge, and the Assize of Bread and Beer, Freedom from Toll thro' all *Cornwal,* two Fairs, the one upon the Eve, Day and Morrow, of St. *Peter in Cathedra,* and the other on the Eve, Day and Morrow, of St. *Barnabas,* and a Weekly Market on *Tuesday,* &c. all which the Burgesses now hold of the said Dutchy in Fee-farm at the Rent of

12*l*. 11*s*. 4*d*. being confirmed by K. *Henry* VIII. 7 *Reg*.

The List of Parliament for this Borough begins the 6th of K. *Edward* VI. and is continued to the 12th of Qu. *Anne.* The present Burgesses, who now serve, are,

The Rt. Hon. *Thomas Cooke* Esq;

Vice-Chamberlain, and

The Hon, *John West* Esq;

11. *Borough of* Eastlow.

IS an ancient Borough and Port, yet not known in any old Grants by this Name, but called either *Loo* simply, or *Portloo.* In the 30th Year of K. *Edward* I. *Henry de Bodrigan* was Lord of this Town, and certified his Claim of a Market and Fair in *Loo,* View of Frank-pledge, a Ducking-Stool, Pillory, and Assize of Bread and Beer. From this Lord the Manor descended to the Family of the *Courtneys,* Earls of *Devon,* who were seiz'd of it the 7th of *Henry* V.

It was made a Corporation by Queen *Elizabeth's* Letters-Patents, bearing Date *January* 8, 1587. by the Name of a Mayor and Burgesses, by which Title they were to have a perpetual Succession, plead, and to be impleaded, and to consist of nine Burgesses, of whom one is always to be Mayor, and to have Power to chuse a Recorder. The Members of Parliament are elected by the Mayor, Burgesses and Freemen, which are about 40 or 50. Before this Charter, the Town was govern'd by a Port-reeve.

The Town contains about 200 Houses, and has a Market on *Saturdays,* of which the Corporation has the Toll. The Manor belongs at present to the Dutchy, and is held by the Corporation at the Fee-farm Rent of *20 s. per Annum.* Here is a poor Battery of four Guns, and a little Chapel of Ease, kept up by four Buttrices, in which the Minister of *St. Martin's,* the Mother-Church and Burial-place, is obliged to preach once in three Weeks. This Chapel was repaired in 1700 by the then Members of Parliament, and afterwards beautified by the present Bishop of *Winchester,* because the Seat of his Family is near this Place. 'Tis dedicated to St. *Kayn* or *Keyna,* an holy Virgin, Daughter of *Braganus,* Prince of *Brecknockshire.* She was anciently in great Esteem for her Holiness in this County and *Somersetshire,* and her Festival is kept on *September* 30, on the Eve of which Day there is a Fair kept in this Town.

The List of the Members of Parliament for this Town begins the 13th of Qu. *Elizabeth,* (for the Return of a Merchant made by this Town, in Conjunction with *Fowey,* to a Council at *Westminster,* must not be reckoned as a Parliament) and is continued down to the 12th Year of Qu. *Anne.* The Burgesses now serving are,

> *John Smith* Esq; and
> *Samuel Bateman* Esq;

12.   *Borough of* Penryn.

I S an ancient Manor belonging to the See of *Exeter,* of which the Corporation now hold it, paying the Bishops a certain Quit-Rent for the Toll of the Markets and Fairs.

The Bishop is Lord of the Borough, and its Forreigns, *i.e.*
Out-Boroughs, it having been made such by *Walter
Bromscomb,* Bishop of *Exeter,* as may appear from the
Petition of *Thomas Button,* Bishop of *Exeter,* who, *Anno*
30 *Edward* I. exhibited his Claim of *Infangthef,* &c. in
his Manor of *Penryn,* which he challenged to be a free
Borough, and to have the Property of a Market and Fair,
and that these Rights were enjoyed by his Predecessors,
who made it a Borough.

The Town consists of one principal Street, indifferently well built for this Country, and hath two Weekly
Markets, which render the Trade considerable, but hath no
Church or Chapel within it ; the Church of *Gluvias,* to
which Parish it belongs, lying but at a quarter of a Mile
distant, tho' *Leland* says, there was a Chapel in the Town
in his Time ; which if true, there are no Signs of it now.

Walter Bronscomb, Bishop of *Exeter* above mentioned, founded a Collegiate Church here for a Dean and
12 Prebendaries, and dedicating it to St. *Mary* and St.
Thomas of *Canterbury,* (as he was in those Days there
esteemed) called it *Glasney* or *Glasneth,* from the Moor
where it was built. It was strongly walled and incastelled,
having three strong Towers, and Guns planted at the End
of the Creek. It was valued at the Dissolution at 205*l.* 12*s.*
6*d.* Part of the Ruins are yet standing, *viz.* a Tower, and
some of the Garden-Walls.

This Town sent Members to Parliament in Qu. *Mary*
and Qu. *Elizabeth's* Reign, but was not incorporated till
Anno 18 of King *James* I. 1619, when, at the Petition of
William Cotton, Bishop of *Exeter,* that King granted,
that it should be a free Borough, consisting of eleven dis-
creet Burgesses or Aldermen, beside a Mayor and twelve

Ccmmon-Council Men, and should have a Recorder, Steward, &c. an Office of Record every three Weeks, a Prison, and Power to try Felons in their Jurisdiction. In the Time of King *James* II. a new Charter was granted to this Corporation, which vested the Election of Members of Parliament in the Magistracy of the Town only ; but it was never made use of. The Election of Burgesses is now made by all the Inhabitants that pay Scot and Lot, who may (perhaps) be estimated it above 100.

The List of the Members of this Town begins the first Year of Qu. *Mary,* and is continued down to the 12th Year of Queen *Anne.* The present Burgesses are,

Samuel Trefusis Esq; and

Hugh Boscawen Esq;

13.   *Borough of* Tregony.

IS mentioned in *Domesday* Book among the Lands of the Earl of *Morton* and *Cornwal,* the Conqueror's Brother, from whom this Manor came very early into the Family of the *Pomeroys,* who by many Descents were found in Possession of it in the 8th Year of Qu. *Elizabeth's* Reign, 1566. From these *Pomeroys* 'tis probable it descended to the *Boscawens* in the Reign of K. *Charles* I. *Hugh Boscawen* being at present the Lord of it, and giving some Sign that he is descended from the *Pomeroys,* because the Christian Name *Hugh* has been so long used in both Families.

This Town consists of one indifferent long Street, and had formerly a Castle in it : but both of them are now much decayed. It has a Parish-Church dedicated to St. *James,* and enjoyed a good Market, till St. *Austel* in the Neighbourhood was made a Market-Town, when it began to decay, and is now inconsiderable, tho' of ancient Date, for *Anno* 30 of K. *Edward* I. *Henry de Pomeroy* before mentioned, then Lord of the Town, certified his Right thereto, together with a Fair, and the Assize of Bread and Beer, and had it allow'd, in which Time also it sent Burgesses to Parliament for two Returns, but no more, till in the Reign of Queen *Elizabeth* it was summoned among the *Cornish* Boroughs, tho' not yet incorporated.

King *James* I. *Anno Reg.* 19, 1620, incorporated this Town by the Title of a Mayor and eight Capital Burgesses, ordaining, That *Tregony* should be a free Borough, consisting of a Mayor and eight Burgesses, who should govern the same ; that they should yearly chuse a Mayor on the *Tuesday* following *Michaelmas*-Day, and have a Recorder, and keep a Court of Record on the first *Monday* of every Month, and enjoy all their ancient Privileges, *&c.*

The Election of Members of Parliament is in the Inhabitants in general, who are all the Housholders that boil the Pot, the Number of which, at a Poll taken in 1695, amounted to about One hundred and fifty.

The List for the Parliament-men mentions the two Returns in K. *Edward's* Days, *Anno Reg.* 23 & 35. but it being discontinued till the first of Queen *Elizabeth,* the continued Catalogue begins the first of *Elizabeth,* and is carried to the 12th Year of Qu. *Anne.* The Burgesses that now serve in Parliament for this Borough are,

Sir *Edmund Prideaux* Bar. and
James Craiggs Jun. Esq;

14. *Borough of* Bossiney.

Ommonly called *Tintagel,* is a small Village, containing not above twenty Houses, and an Hamlet with *Trevena* to that Parish. The Manor is Very ancient Demesne Land to the Crown, and famous in our Histories for a Castle, the Ruins of which are reckon'd one of the Wonders of the World, standing about half a Mile from these Towns, part on the Continent, and part on an Island, joined together by a Draw-bridge. It had in it a pretty Chapel dedicated to St. *Julian,* as the Parish-Church is to St. *Simphorian.* The Church of *Tintagel* was impropriated to the College of *Windsor* by the Gift of *Edward* IV. who granted the Advowson of it to that College by his Letters Patents, dated *June* 29, 1480. *Reg* 40.

Richard Earl of *Cornwal,* Brother to King *Henry* III. procured a Grant from that King, *Quod Burgas noster de Tyntaivil sit Liber Burgus, i.e.* That *Tyntaivil* should be a free Borough. It is govern'd by a Mayor, but so far as we can discover not incorporated. The first Return of Members we can find is in King *Edward* VI.'s Reign. In the Indenture in Qu. *Mary's* Time, it is called *Trevena,* alias *Bossiney,* and sometimes one of them alone. The Election of Members is in the Mayor and Freemen. Whoever has free Land in the Borough, and lives in the Parish, is a Freeman, and votes in all Elections of the Mayor and Burgesses. The Number of Electors is said to be under twenty.

The Castle, Manor and Borough of *Tintagel,* was

settled by King *Edward* III. on his Son the Black Prince,
when he created him Duke of *Cornwal,* and his Heirs the
Princes of the Blood for ever, and so 'tis become a Parcel
of that Dutchy, and as such is held by the Corporation, at
the Fee-farm Rent of 11*l.* 16*s.* 9*d. per Ann.* The Castle is
said to be a very ancient Building, and to have been the
Seat of the Dukes of *Cornwal* in the Times of the *Britains,* and (as some pretend) the Birth place of King
Arthur, 500 Years before the Conquest ; but now only the
Ruins of some Works remain.

The List of the Parliament-men begins in *Edward*
IV.'s Reign, *6 Reg* and is continued to the 12th Year of
Qu. *Anne.* The present Representatives of this Place are,

Henry Cartwright Esq; and

Samuel Molineux Esq;

15.   *Borough of* St. Ives.

Akes its Name from an *Irish* Saint, St. *Jia,* a Noble-
man's Daughter of *Ireland,* famous for her singular
Sanctity, who came hither about the Year 460, having
been a Disciple of St. *Barricus,* first Bishop of *Cork* ; so
that the true Name of the Town is *St. Jies,* and corruptly
called *St. Ives,* (as it is commonly call'd and nam'd in the
Maps.)

It is a neat Town for this County. The Inhabitants
are wealthy, and have twenty Sail of Ships or more
belonging to their Harbour. They drive a great Pilchard-
Trade in the Bay. The Church is wide and capacious, but
low, having a handsome Tower, a Nave, and two Iles. The

great Tithes of the whole Parish of *Unilalant,* of which this Town is but an Hamlet, are impropriate, and vested in the Earl of *Stamford,* who takes Tithes not only of Grain, but of Fish, Lamb and Wool, so that little is left to the Vicar but the Tenth of Hay, Milk and Mortuaries ; which last, tho' used in few Places else in *England,* bring in a considerable Revenue ; for the Custom is this, That whoever dies worth 10*l.* or more, pays 10*s.* to the Vicar ; but they that die worth less, pay nothing, and the richest no more.

The Manor was anciently in the Family of the *Ferrers,* from whom it came by Marriage to the *Champernoons,* and from them in the same manner to Sir *Robert Willoughby,* Lord *Brooke,* whose Coheiresses marrying to *Blunt* Lord *Mountjoy,* and Mr. *Paulet,* it came upon the Division to this latter, who held it in the Reign of K. *Charles* I. being the Ancestor of the present Duke of *Polton.* It continues still in that Family, he being Lord of it.

When it was made a Borough, we can't understand. In the last Parliament of Queen *Mary,* two Burgesses were sent to Parliament for the Borough of *St. Ise,* which we believe to be this Town, and then 'twas called a Borough, and said to be govern'd by a Portreeve. It was incorporated by King *Charles* I. *Anno Reg.* 16, 1641, who by his Charter grants, That the Borough and Parish of *St. Ives* should be incorporated, have a Common-Seal, be govern'd by a Mayor, 12 Capital and 24 inferior Burgesses, a Recorder, Town-Clerk, *&c.* of which the Mayor in his Office, and a Year after, the Senior Burgess and Recorder, shall be always Justices of the Peace ; That they shall have four Fairs, *viz.* on *May* 10, *July* 20, *September*

26, and *December 3,* and a Day after each of them ; and two Markets, *viz,* on *Wednesday* and *Saturday,* and a Grammar-School for the Instruction of Youth by a Master and Usher, of which the Bishop of *Exeter,* Mayor and Capital Burgesses for the Time being, are appointed Governors.

The Election of the Members for Parliament is made by the Corporation, and all the Inhabitants that pay Scot and Lot, which are in all about 180. The Corporation now pays to the Duke of *Bolton* a Fee-farm Rent of 13*s.* 4*d.* and an high Rent of 1*s.* 2*d.* for the Market-House.

The List of the Members of this Borough begins the 4th and 5th of K. *Philip* and Q. *Mary,* and is continued to the 12th Year of Qu. *Anne.* The present Burgesses are,

The Hon. *Henry Pawlet* Esq; and

Sir *John Hobart* Bar.

16.   *Borough of* Fowey.

IS a very ordinary Town, the Buildings being ill contriv'd, and so confusedly crowded together, that there is no open Street belonging to it, only many intricate Passages. The Church, dedicated to S. *Fimbarrus,* commonly called *Barrus,* first Bishop of *Cork* in *Ireland,* is a pretty large Building, but something clumsy and inartificial. It was erected in the Reign of K. *Henry* VI. or K. *Edward* IV. by the Earl of *Warwick,* and in it is a Table of Benefactors hanging, of which Mr. *Vincent,* who gave 30*l. per Ann.* to the Free-School, and Mr. *Rashleigh,* who endowed an Hospital here, are the most eminent.

The Manor was given by the Conqueror to *Robert* Earl of *Morton* and *Cornwal,* and afterwards, in *Richard* I.'s Reign, settled by *Robert de Cardinan* upon the Priory of *Tywardresh,* which he founded in the Neighbourhood. In the Reign of K. *Edward* I. the Prior of this House certified his Claim of Assize of Bread and Beer and View of Frank-pledge in *Fowey,* and in the next Reign the Convent obtain'd a Grant of a *Monday* Market weekly at the Manor of *Fawe,* and two Fairs annually, *viz.* on the Eve, Day and Morrow, of St. *Barrus,* and on the Eve, Day and Morrow, of St. *Lucy.* The Priory held it till the Dissolution by K. *Henry* VIII. when it was annexed to the Dutchy ; but the Toll and Toldsey of the Market and Fairs, and Keyage of the Harbour, were vested in the Corporation, upon the Payment of a Fee-farm Rent of 1*l.* 19*s. 2d. per Ann.* to the Dutchy.

When this Town was made a Borough, we can't learn ; but certain it is, that it never returned any Members to Parliament before the 13th Year of Queen *Elizabeth* ; tho' in K. *Edward* III.'s Days it sent a Merchant, with *Eastlow,* to a Council at *Westminster,* to treat of Sea-Affairs, as is above mentioned.

The Harbour of this Town is very commodious for Shipping, the Entrance being narrow, but very deep for three Miles to return into the Country, and all the Ways very clear from Bars of Sand and Rocks. At the Mouth of the Harbour, on the West Side, are the Ruins of an old Castle, and when you have passed a little farther, two small square Towers, opposite the one to the other, from which, in the last *Dutch* War, there was a Chain extending 200 Foot long ; but 'tis now lost.

The Corporation consists of a Mayor, eight Aldermen, and two Assistants, and the Burgesses are chosen by all the Inhabitants that pay Scot and Lot. The Mayor in his Office, and the next Year after, and the Senior Alderman, always Justices of the Peace. King *James* II. allowed them a Recorder.

The List of Parliament-men begins *Anno* 13. *Eliz,* and ends at the 12th of Qu. *Anne.* The present Members are,

> *Henry Vincent Jun.* Esq; and
> *Jonathan Elford* Esq;

17.   *Borough of* St. Germans.

TAkes its Name from St. *German,* a Native, and at last Bishop of *Auxerre* in *France,* who being a great Orator, was sent into *England* to oppose the *Pelagian* Heresy by the *French* Bishops, and after he had preached in divers Parts of the Kingdom, as *Verulam, Wales,* &c. with good Success, took up his Residence here for some time. In Memory, of him, K. *Athelstan* built here a fair Church ; and because the Bishops of *Cornwal,* who resided then at *Bodmin,* were much molested by the *Danes,* he removed the See to this Town, where it continued during the Succession of ten Bishops, *viz.* 113 Years, and then was removed to *Exeter* by *Leofricus,* who changed the Secular Canons put in by K. *Athelstan* into Black Canons.

The Manor of this Town, which (as *Domesday*-Book informs us) consisted of 24 Hides of Land, was upon this Change divided between the Bishop of *Exeter* and the

Convent, 12 being given to each, but not of equal Value, for the Bishop's Part was then valued at 8*l. per Ann.* and the Monks at 5*l.* only. Here was then a Market on the Lord's-Day, but soon came to nothing, because the Earl of *Morton* encouraged the Market at *Trematon,* where his Castle was. The Division of the Manor still continues, *Edward Elliot* Esq; who farms the Bishop's Part, and possesses the other from his Ancestors, who bought it of the *Champernoons,* to whom it came accidentally at the Dissolution, enjoying both distinctly, and from them the Place where the Priory stood is called *Port-Elliot.*

The Town is ruinous and poor, the Houses are meanly built and irregular, situate upon an uneven Rock, affording no tolerable Reception for Passengers or Travellers. The Market, which it pretends to, and endeavours to keep up, is on *Fridays,* but is small, peddling, and almost unfrequented. All the Trade it drives is by fishing in *Tiddiford* River, which passes by the Town, and about 10 Miles lower empties it self into *Plimouth* Harbour. The Priory, being the Mansion of Mr. *Elliot,* is an handsome large Building, and fronts to the River. In the great Hall are the Arms of the Priory, in the painted Glass of a large Bow-Window, *viz.* a Sword and two Keys, endorsed in *Saltire.* The Church stands near the Priory, and consists of a North Ile, and two spacious Naves. At the West End were two lofty Towers, but now near demolished. The Naves before the Dissolution were appointed the one for the Convent, and the other for the Parishioners ; but since they are both laid together. The whole is a light, handsome Building, and in it are divers Monuments of the *Moyles,* and a Marble one of one Mr. *Scawen.* The Presentation of the Vicaridge of this Town, and Impropriation or Rectory, were by. King *Edward* VI. granted to the Dean and Chapter of *Windsor,* in whose Hands they remain at this Day.

When this Town was made a Borough, is not known ; but the first Return of Burgesses which we find was 5 *Eliz.* and then made by their Portreeve or Mayor, who is chosen at the Lord's Court-Leet, held about *Michaelmas,* by a Jury impanelled by the Steward for that purpose. The Members of Parliament are chosen by all the Housholders that have lived a Year within the Borough, which contains only 50 or 60 Houses near the Church, the rest of the Parish, which is the largest in *Cornwal,* (being 20 Miles in Compass, and has 10 Hamlets, in which are divers Gentlemens Seats) being without the Borough.

The List of the Members of Parliament begins the 5th of Qu. *Elizabeth,* and ends at the 12th Year of Qu. *Anne.* The present Representatives are,

> *John Bacon* Esq; and
> *John Knight* Esq;

18.   *Borough of* St. Michael.

IS a small Hamlet, made up of Cottages, save one House, which is a publick Inn, not long since erected, and is the only tiled House in the Borough, which has not 30 more. It is a Thoroughfair, and one Side of it lies in the Parish of *Newlyn,* and the other of St. *Enodore,* so called from an *Irish* Saint.

The Manor of this Town is still in the Possession of the *Arundels* of *Llhanhern,* whose Ancestor *Ralph de*

Arundel, executing the Office of Sheriff in this County for *Richard* Earl of *Cornwal,* King of the *Romans,* procured the Privileges for this Town of being a Borough, and having a Market and Fair ; which last is still kept on St. *Francis's* Day, on the 4th of *October.*

This Borough is govern'd by a Portreeve, annually elected at the Court-Leet of the Heir of *Arundel* of *Llanhern,* the present High-Lord, by a Jury, consisting of the principal Inhabitants of the Borough. The Portreeve must be chosen out of the six chief Tenants, called Deputy-Lords, because they have Lands in the Borough, who are at this time, Sir *Richard Carew,* Sir *Richard Vivian,* Bar[ts]. Sir *William Scawen* Kt, *Hugh Boscawen,* and *William Courtney,* Esqs; and - - - - *Gully,* Gent, and no other is capable of that Office. There is no Chapel in this little Town of *Modishole,* as 'tis called, 30 *Edw.* I. neither can we learn that there ever was any.

We can't find that it was ever incorporated, but that it sent Members to Parliament the 6th of K. *Edward* VI. in which Return it is called, as also in other Indentures, *Burgus & Villa Mychel, Mitchel,* or *Modishole,* and no where *St. Michael,* till of late it has been termed so by vulgar Error. The Election of Burgesses to serve in Parliament has been made here several ways, *viz.* sometimes by a Jury of the principal Inhabitants, and at other times by the Inhabitants in general, which causing some Contests among the People, the House of Commons, by Vote *March* 20, 1700. settled the Election for the future to be performed by the Lords of the Borough capable of being Portreeves, and such Inhabitants as pay Scot and Lot, which are not now above 26.

The List of the Parliament-men begins the 6th Year

of K. *Edward* VI. and ends at the 12th Year of Qu. *Anne.* The present Burgesses are,

Nathaniel Blackiston Esq; and
Richard Molesworth Esq;

19. *Borough of* Newport.

IS so called of late Years from a New Gate, in Latin *Nova Porta,* built to it. It is part of the Parish of *St. Stephens,* and grew into a Town or Suburb to *Launceston,* upon the Removal of the Priory Church, which occasioning a Church or Chapel, now known by the Name of St. *Thomas,* to be erected in its room, certain Houses were built about it, which are now about 80, and are all comprized in the Borough of *Newport,* formerly called *Dunheven,* as well as *Launceston.*

The Manor of this Hamlet belonged to the Priors of St. *Stephen,* as *Launceston* did to the Earls and Dukes of *Cornwal,* as appears by *Domesday*-Book, which tells us, that *Canonici, &c. i.e.* The Canons of St. *Stephen* hold *Lanstaveton* ; and then adds, *Comes, &c.* The Earl of *Morton* holds *Dunhevet,* where he hath a Castle ; which different Tenures, as they divided this Place into Ecclesiastical and Lay Possessions, and on that account were separated in Jurisdiction, so they obtained distinct Privileges, which this Place laid Claim to at the Dissolution. This part of the Manor then devolved to the Crown, and so continued, till King *Charles* II. upon his Restoration, gave it to Sir *William Morrice,* in whose Family it still remains, Sir *Nicholas Morrice* being now Lord of the Manor and Borough of *Newport.*

It does not appear from any ancient Records, that this Place was ever incorporated, or so much as stiled a Borough ; yet being part of the King's Demesnes, it speciously challenged a Right to return Members to Parliament the 6th of *Edward* VI. and sending their Burgesses, they were admitted, and have exercised the same Privilege ever since. They have a Custom to chuse two Persons yearly, called *Vianders,* at the Lord's Court, who are the Officers that order their Elections, and make the Returns of the Representatives, who are chosen by all the Inhabitants of the Place who pay Scot and Lot, or have Burgage-Tenure in this District, which are about 60 in Number.

The List of the Burgesses for this Town begins the 6th of K. *Edward VI.* and is continued to the 12th Year of Qu. *Anne.* The present Members are,

Sir *Nicholas Morrice* Bar. and

Humphrey Morrice Esq;

20.　*Borough of* St. Mawes.

IS a small Hamlet, containing about the same Number of Houses as *St. Michael* above mentioned, and has neither Church nor Chapel, but belongs to the Parish of St. *Justus,* who left his Bishoprick of *Lyons,* and turn'd Hermit. The Name of this Place is derived from an *Irish* Saint of that Name, who had his Cell here, and lived in great Abstinence, which occasion'd a Church to be built here to his Memory, and that a Fisher-Town to rise up after it.

K. *Henry* VIII. built a Castle here to secure the

Entrance of *Falmouth* Harbour. It was of an orbicular Form, but of little Strength, which makes it little regarded, and so is not kept in good Repair ; yet there are belonging to it a Governor, who has a Salary of about 80*l. per Ann.* a Deputy, who has about 26*l. per Ann.* and two Gunners, who attend by Turns, for there are about 17 Guns belonging to it.

The Manor and Royalty belonged, 'tis probable, to the Crown, till within this last Century it was sold to Sir *Joseph Tredenham,* whose Relict now enjoys it for Life ; after which it descends to *Francis Scobell* Esq; who married the Daughter of the said Sir *Joseph,* who died about 10 Years since.

This Town never sent any Members to Parliament till the Year 1562, 5 *Eliz.* when being accepted, on Condition that they should shew their Letters-Patents for their Return, which were never required, they have accordingly sent ever since. The chief Officer of the Borough is a Portreeve or Mayor, who with the free and sworn Tenants, who are about 30 or 40 in Number, having elected their Burgesses, makes a Return of them. We do not find that it was ever incorporated, or had either Market or Fair. The Inhabitants depend chiefly upon Fishing for their Subsistence.

The List of the Parliament-men for this Town begins 5 *Eliz.* and is continued to the 12th Year of Qu. *Anne.* The Burgesses that now serve in Parliament are,

William Lowndes Esq; and

John Chetwind Esq;

21. *Borough of* Kellington.

THO' the last of the Boroughs of this County in Order of Time, yet for Building and Wealth is not inferior to above half of them, containing above 150 Houses. The Manor of this Town was in King *Henry* III's Time the Estate of *Reginald de Ferrers,* and his Heirs ; for we find, that that King granted him a Market every *Wednesday* at his Manor of *Calweton* in *Com. Cornwal,* and a fair annually on the Eve, Day and Morrow, of the Nativity of the Virgin *Mary* ; which being on *September* 8 it is here kept on the Anniversary of the Dedication of the Chapel of this Town, which is a Daughter-Church (as they call it) to the Parish of *Southill,* distant about two Miles. It is probable this *Reginald* held it at first of *Richard* Earl of *Cornwal,* who made it a Borough by Lease, to pay certain Rents and Services, which were continued in K. *Edward* III.'s Days. From the Family of the *Ferrers,* it came by Marriage to the *Champernoons,* and from them to the Lord *Willoughby* of *Brooke,* then to the *Paulets,* Marquisses of *Winchester,* by a Daughter of whom it descended to Sir *Henry Rolle* ; of *Stevenston, Devon,* whose Posterity now enjoy it. Here is a good Market-House, and a neat Chapel or Church dedicated to St. *Mary,* but made such by the Piety of *Nicholas de Ashton,* Serjeant at Law, who in a great measure rebuilt it, and lies buried in the Chancel, under a Marble Monument.

The inhabitants have no Charter of Incorporation,

but every Year at the Court-Leet of the Lord of the Manor, who is at present *Samuel Rolle* Esq; the Portreeve is chosen, and the Inhabitants who have lived in it a Twelvemonth are admitted Burgesses, which gives them a Right to vote at the Elections of Members of Parliament, so that there are almost as many Electors as Houses. The Returning Officer is the Portreeve, by Prescription. The first Return of Members to Parliament made by this Borough was *27 Eliz.* 1585, it being the last Town in *Cornwal* that was called upon to send Representatives.

The List of Parliament-men for this Borough begins the 27th Year of Qu. *Elizabeth,* and ends the 12th Year of Qu. *Anne.* The present Members are,

Sir *John Coriton* Bar. and
Samuel Rolle Esq;

Gazetteer

ABO	Hundred	Deanery	Valuation	Patron	Incumbent
Aborrows	Kerryer				
Advene	Lesnewth	Trigg Minor	————	Chapel annexed to *Lanteglos* by *Camelford*	
St. Agnes	Pider				
St. Allen	Powder	V. Powder	8 13 4	Ld. Bp. of *Exon*	Mr. *Wi. Richards*
Allercomb	Stratton				
Alternon	Lesnewth	V. Trigg Major	18 4 10½	D. & C. of *Exon*	*L. Blackburne* D.D.
Andenos Castle	Pider				
Anowthan	Penwith				
Anstel	Powder				
Anthony	Powder				
Anthony East	East				
Anthony Hall	East				
St. Anthony in Meney	Kerryer	V. Kerryer	4 15 11½	The Crown	*John Taylor* Vic.
Anthony West	East	V. East	12 17 8½	Sir *W. Carew* Bar.	*John Taylor* Vic.
Anthron	Kerryer				
Ardenora	Powder				
Armed Knight	Penwith				
Arthur's Hall	Trigg				
Arwanack	Kerryer				
Arwothal	Kerryer				
Asalt	East				
Ashfield	Powder				
St. AUSTEL o=	Powder	V. Powder	21 0 0	The Crown	*Step. Hewgoe* Vic.
Bake	East	V. Kerryer	33 0 0	The Crown	*H. Huthnanse* Vic.
Barret	Powder				
Barton Bickton	East				
Barton Trenew	East				
Bedeve	Trigg				
Bedwin	Trigg				
Benallock	Kerryer				
Benallock	Powder				
St. Bennet	Pider				
Beny	Lesnewth				
Bere	Stratton				
Berion	East				
Besill	Lesnewth				
Betonet	East				
Bickton	East				
Bindon	West				
Binerton	Kerryer				
St. Blaise	Powder	Powder	————	Chapel annexed to *St. Austell.*	
Blisland	Trigg	R. Trigg Min.	13 10 0	Mr *Nich. Parsons*	Vacant.
Blostenhim	East				
Bochyn	Kerryer				
Boconock	West	R. West	9 17 8	Lady *Eliz. Mohun*	*Cha. Peters* Rect.
Bockonock Hall	West				
BODMIN o=	Trigg	V. Trigg Min.	13 6 8	Sir *P. Prideaux* B	*Jasper Wood* Vic.

BOD	Hundred	Deanery	Valuation	Patron	Incumbent
Bodregan	Powder				
Bodrigy	Penwith				
Bodwell	West				
Bolisto	Penwith				
Bollytho	East				
Bonython	Kerryer				
Borden	Stratton				
Borrow	Stratton				
BOSCASTLE o=	Lesnewth				
Boskenna	Penwith				
Bosvergus	Penwith				
Botadon	East				
Botalleck	Penwith				
Botesflening	East	East		*Ed. Herle* of *Prideaux* Es^{qs} *R. Killiow* of *Landleak,*	*Arthur Pearse,* Cl.
Botsboro	Stratton				
Boyton	Stratton	Trigg Major	——	.... *Langford.*	Impropriation, *Ch. Hawke,* Cur.
Breage	Kerryer				
Bren	Pider				
St. Brecknock	Pider	R. Pider	41 10 8	Sir *N. Morrice* Bar.	*Ch. Pole,* Rect.
St. Breward *alias* Symon Ward	Trigg	V. Trigg Minor	8 0 0	D. & C. of *Exon.*	*Nich. Downe,* Vic.
Brodock	West	V. West	8 13 4	*Sam. Cabel* Esq;	*Thos. Pearse,* Vic.
Broungelly	West				
Brown-Willow	East				
Buckern	Trigg				
Buckley	Trigg				
Budock	Kerryer				
Burgus	Pider				
St. Burien	Penwith	R. Penwith	48 12 0	Bp. of *Exon, as* D. of *S. Burien*	... *Edwards,* Cur. no Institution.
Burlase	Penwith				
Burnere	Trigg				
Burton	East				
Bynaway	Stratton				
Bynith Wood	East				
Calstock	East				
Camborn	Penwith	Penwith	39 16 10½	*Fran. Bassett* Esq;	*J. Newcombe,* Rect.
CAMELFORD o=	Lesnewth				
Canalegie	Pider				
Canyieke	Penwith				
Carantock	Pider	Pider	Chapel annex'd to *Padstow*		*Steph. Warne,* Cur.
Cardingham	West	R. West	24 17 8½	*Ed. Herle, J. Grove* Esqs; *alt. vic.*	*John Baker,* Rect.
Cardock	West				
Cargallomb	West				
Cargeren	East				
Carlogus	Pider				
Carminow	Kerryer				
Carnon	Pider				
Carnonbigh	Penwith				
Carrock Passage	West				

CAS	Hundred	Deanery	Valuation	Patron	Incumbent
Casthorn	Penwith				
Cayne	West				
Chasfell	East				
Cleader	Lesnewth	V. Trigg Major	6 11 10½		
St. Cleather *al.* Cleader	———	Trigg Major	———	*John Trevillian* Esq;	*John Harris,* Vic.
St. Cleere	West	V. West	19 6 8	The Crown	*Edw. Dennis,* Vic.
St. Clement	Powder	Powder	9 0 0	The Crown	*Samuel Ange,* Vic.
Clifton	East				
Clowant	Penwith				
Colan Parva	Pider	V. Pider	6 14 4	Bishop of *Exon.*	*Jo. Baggwell,* Vic.
Collostock	East	East	———	The Crown	*L. Blackburne,* D.D.
Colquite	Powder				
Columb John	Pider				
COLUMB MAGNA o=	Pider	R. Pider	53 6 8	*John Collier,* Cl.	*Phil. Collier,* Rect.
Columb Parva	Pider	Pider	———	———	*P. Hill,* Cur. Impr.
Comb	Powder				
Constenton	Kerryer	V. Kerryer	19 3 10½	D. & C. of *Exon.*	*Tho. Perry,* Vic.
Corneley	Powder	V. Powder	19 0 0	Chapel annex'd to *Probus.*	
Correther	West				
Coswyn	Penwith				
Coutt	Powder				
Crackington	Lesnewth				
Creed	Powder	R. Powder	13 6 8	The Crown.	*John Hughs,* Rect.
Crigmere	Pider				
Crocabon	East				
Crowan	Penwith				
Crowan Hall	Penwith	V. Penwith	11 9 ½	*S. Aubyn* Esq;	*John Glynn,* Vic.
Cubly	Powder				
Culverland	West				
Curbeal	East				
Curry	Kerryer	Kerryer	Chapel annex'd to *Breague*		
Cuswath	Pider				
Cuthbert, *al.* Cubert	Pider	V. Pider	8 6 8	Sir *P. Prideaux* B!	*Hu. Bradford,* Vic.
Cutmere	East				
Davidstow, *al.* Davstowe	Lesnewth	V. Trigg Major	8 0 0	The Crown.	*N. Tincombe,* Vic.
St. Daye	Kerryer				
Denisak	West				
Denner Bridge	Trigg				
St. Denis	Powder	Powder	Chapel annex'd to *St. Michael Caryhays*		
St. Dominick	East	R. East	23 11 ½	*John Clarke* Esq;	*Joseph Clarke.*
Dulo	West	R. West	22 4 0	Master & Scholars of *Baliol* College, *Oxon.*	*Jo. Baron,* S.T.P.
Dulo	West	V. West	8 11 ½	Rector of the Rect. of *Dulo.*	*Jerem. Mills,* Vic.
Dyzard	Lesnewth				
Efford	Stratton				
Eglorouse	East				
Egloshale	Trigg	V. Trigg Minor	16 0 0	Ld. Bp. of *Exon.*	*Jo. Hathaway,* Vic.
Eglos-Kerry	East	Trigg Major	———	The Crown.	Impropriation *Geo. Jagce,* Cur.
Endellion	Trigg	R. Trigg Minor	10 0 0	The Crown.	*Jona. Dagg,* Rect.
St. Enedor	Pider	V. Pider	26 13 4	Bishop of *Exon.*	*Sam. Martyn,* Vic.

ENI	Hundred	Deanery	Valuation	Patron	Incumbent
Enis, *al* Gennis	Kerryer	V. Trigg Major	8 0 0	E. Eliott, of Port-Elliott, J. Molesworth, of Pencarrow, Esqs;	Rich. Crews, Vic.
St. Ercy, *al* Earth	Penwith	V. Penwith	————	Dean & Chapter of Exon.	John Ralph, Vic.
Erghe	Penwith	V. Penwith	14 1 ½		
Erme	Powder	R. Powder	22 13 4	Na. Lutterell, Gent.	Fr. Carthew, Rect.
Ervan	Pider	R. Pider	18 6 8	Sir Nic. Morrice.	John Day, Rect.
Ethy, *al* S. Issie	West	V. Pider	9 0 0	D. & C. of Exon.	Philip Sprey, Vic.
Eva, *al* S. Tue	Powder	R. Powder	21 0 0	Sir Jos. Tredenham.	Jo. Penneck, Rect.
Evall	Pider	V. Pider	6 13 4	Bishop of Exon.	Jth. Bagwell, Vic.
FAL- MOUTH o=	Kerryer				
Falstow	East				
Feock	Powder	V. Powder	11 0 0	Bishop of Exon.	Sam. Ange, Vic.
Forybery	Lesnewth	R. Trigg Minor	4 12 8½	Sir John Cotton.	James Amy, Rect.
FOWEY o=	Powder	V. Powder	10 0 0	Tho. Trefry, Gent.	Jonat. Dagg, Vic.
Frisey	Kerryer				
Garbine	Penwith				
Gennis					
St. Germans	Lesnewth				
Germor	Kerryer	V. Powder	20 0 0	No Institution.	Mr Kendall, Cur.
Gerrance	Powder	R. Powder	15 12 6	Bishop of Exon.	J. Trenhayle, Rect.
Giles in the Heath	————	Trigg Major	————	The Crown.	Impropriation J. Braddon, Cur.
Gillet	Lesnewth				
Gluvius	Kerryer	V. Kerryer	21 6 9	Bishop of Exon.	John Collyer, Vic.
Glyford	West				
Glyman	Pider				
Guarnack	Powder				
Godolphin	Kerryer				
Godolphin Hall	Kerryer				
Goland	Powder				
Golden	Powder				
Golsury	Penwith				
Goran	Powder	Powder	20 0 0	Bishop of Exon.	John Shapler, Vic.
Grade	Kerryer	R. Kerryer	11 1 5½	J. Trevanion, of Caryhays, Esq;	Philip Pyne, Rect.
GRAM- POND o=	Powder				
Grendon	Kerryer				
Greston	East				
Gulvall	Penwith	V. Penwith	6 11 6	The Crown.	J. Penhellick, Vic.
Gunhaskin	Pider				
Gunwallow	Kerryer	Kerryer	Chapel annex'd to *Breague*.		
Gurran	Powder				
Gwynap	Kerryer	Kerryer	16 10 1½	D. & C. of Exon.	James Bishop, Vic.
Gwyniei	Penwith				
Gwynnear	————	Penwith	————	Bishop of Exon.	Tho. Paynter, Vic.
Gwythion	Penwith	Penwith	Chapel annex'd to *Phyllack*.		
Hackton	East				
Hale	East				
Hall	West				

HAL	Hundred	Deanery	Valuation	Patron	Incumbent
Hall Drunkard	Lesnewth				
Hall-win	Pider				
Ham	Stratton				
Harlyne	Pider				
Harnaborough	East				
Haye	East				
Helland	Trigg	R. Trigg Minor	9 13 4	*R. Hele,* of *Fleet,*Esq;	*Ed. White,* Rect.
Hellegan	Trigg				
Helset	Lesnewth				
HELSTON o=	Kerryer	V. Kerryer	26 19 3	*Wa. Jagoe,* of *Dartmouth, Henry Dottyn,* of *Sherford,* Gent.	*John Jagoe,* Vic.
Helston ford	East				
Helwin	Pider				
Heple-Mill	East				
Hillary (St.)	Penwith	V. Penwith	11 6 0½	Sir *Will. Godolphin.*	*Jo. Penneck,* Vic.
Hilton	Stratton				
Hussan	Pider				
Jacobstow	Stratton	R. Trigg Maj.	19 0 0	*Mary Rashly,* Wid.	*Jeff. Lupton,* Rect.
Janus	Powder	V. Powder	10 4 0	Chapel annex'd to *Tregony.*	
Ilcomb	Stratton	R. Penwith			
Illogan	Penwith	Penwith	22 7 5	*Fran. Bassett* Esq;	*R. Newcombe,* Rect.
St. John's	East	R. East	12 12 4	The Crown.	Mr *John Torr.*
St. John's	Kerryer				
St. Issey	Pider				
St. Ives	East	R. East	26 0 0	The Crown.	*John Bagwell,* Rect.
ST. IVES o=	Penwith	Penwith	Chapel annex'd to *Unilalant.*		
St. Julyett	——	Trigg Major	——	. . . *Molesworth.*	Impropriation *N. Tincombe,* Cu.
St. Just	Penwith	V. Penwith	11 11 0½	The Crown.	*Jam. Millett,* Vic.
St. Just	Powder	R. Powder	37 0 10	*J. Tredenham, Rich. Jack,* Esqs;	*T. Woolridge,* Rect.
St. Just Castle	Powder				
Karnusack	Penwith				
St. Kayne	West	R. West	5 18 6	*Jo. Cory,* of *Pancrasweek,* Gent.	*John Harris,* Rect.
Keby	Powder				
Kellah	Penwith				
KELLING- TON o=	East				
Kennegy	Penwith				
Kenwyne	Powder	V. Powder	16 0 0	Bishop of *Exon.*	*Will. Michell,* Vic.
Kergo	Pider				
Kernbray	Penwith				
Kerneth	Powder				
Kernsew	Kerryer				
Kestle	Kerryer				
Keswell	Trigg				
Kewart	West				
St. Kevern	Kerryer	V. Kerryer	18 11 4½	*Rich. Hele,* Esq;	*R. Woodford,* Vic.
St. Kewe	Trigg				
Key	Powder				
Kibberd	Pider	V. Pider	8 6 8	*See* Cuthbert, *alias* Cubert.	
Kicklow	Kerryer				

KEW	Hundred	Deanery	Valuation	Patron	Incumbent
St. Kew, *al.* Lanew	———	Trigg Major.	19 11 0½	*J. Tregeagle*, Gent.	*John Nations*, Vic.
Kilguth	Penwith				
Kilkhampton	Stratton	R. Trigg Maj.	26 3 10½	*Geo. Granville* Esq;	*C. Granville*, Rect.
Kilkhampton	Stratton				
Killegate	West				
Killew	Powder				
King's Preb. *al.* Bodmin Preb. *founded in the Ch. of* Endellion.	———	Trigg Minor.	———	*John Bassett* Esq;	*Gilb. Langon*, Rect.
Kirthies	Penwith				
St. Knett	Lesnewth	V. Trigg Minor	19 10 0		
Ladock	Powder	R. Powder	18 0 0	{ *Pet. Courtney*, of *Trethurfe*, Esq;	*Will. Wood*, Rect.
Lalant	Penwith				
Uni-Lalant	Penwith	V. Penwith	22 11 10½	Bishop of *Exon.*	*W. Pelkinkerne*, V.
Lam-chane	West				
Lammoram	Powder	R. Powder	6 0 0	{ *Will. Sparke*, of *Friory*, Esq;	*Vau. Kestell*, Rect.
Lanbrigan	Pider				
Lanbrize	Pider				
Landew	East				
Landewenake	Kerryer	R. Kerryer	11 16 8½	*Geo. Robinson* Esq;	*Will. Robinson*, R.
Landilp	East	R. East	20 3 6	The Crown.	Mr *Jobe Brookes.*
Laneathow	West	R. West	32 0 0	*Cha. Grills* Esq;	*Nich. Grills*, Rect.
Lanest	———	Trigg Major.	———	The Crown.	Impr. *J. Harris*, R.
Langdon	Stratton				
Langford	Stratton				
Langhadern	Powder				
Langham	Pider				
Lanhedwick	Pider	Trigg Minor.	———	Earl of *Radnor.*	*J. Baker*, C. Impr.
Lanhedwick House	Pider				
Lanivet	Pider	R. Pider	24 0 0	*Anth. Nicholls* Esq;	*Jam. Vashon*, Rect.
Lanliveri	Powder	V. Powder	13 6 8	*Walt. Kendall* Esq;	*Nic. Kendall*, Vic.
Lanno	Trigg				
Lanrack	East	R. East	18 12 4	*Ed. Nosworthy* Esq;	*Phil. Wynell*, Vic.
Lanreth	West				
Lansallos	West	R. West	18 0 0	*Rich. Killiowe* Esq;	*Ja. Cunning*, R.
Lanteglass *and* Advent	Lesnewth	R. Trigg Minor	34 11 2½	The Crown.	*H. Whiteans*, Rect.
Lanteglass *by* Foy	West	R. West	14 7 2½	Sir *Art. Harris* Esq;	*R. Perkinson*, Vic.
Launce	Powder				
Launsells	Stratton	R. Trigg Maj.	10 10 8½	*Paul Orchard* Esq;	*Tho. Orchard*, Vic.
LAUNCESTON o=	East	Trigg Major.	———	The Crown.	Mr *Sa. Boughton*
Launceston Castle	East				
St. Lawrence	Trigg				
Lawannick	East	V. East	7 18 2	The Crown.	Mr *Ely Foster*
Lawhitton	East	R. East	19 6 8	Bishop of *Exon.*	*Tim. Shute*, Rect.
Lawreth	West				
Lean Castle	East				

LEE	Hundred	Deanery	Valuation			Patron	Incumbent
Lee	Stratton						
Lepperry	Pider						
Lesante	East	R. East	32	0	0	Bishop of *Exon.*	*H. Austen,* DD. R.
LESKARD o=	West	V. West	18	13	10	{ *Jos. Calmady* of *Wembury* Esq;	*Pet. Osborne,* Vic.
Lesnewth	Lesnewth	R. Trigg Minor	8	0	0	*Al. Tregian,* Gent.	*Chr. Tregian,* Rect.
Lestorman	Powder	V. Powder	2	13	4		
LESTWI- THIEL o=	Powder	Powder	————				
Letkee Dineck	East						
Levan	Penwith						
Levethan	Trigg						
Lezard	Kerryer						
Lezard-Point	Kerryer						
Linkenhorn	East	V. East	13	0	0	{ *Mag. Vacy,* Widow of *Vacy.*	*Fran. Byne,* Cl.
Lisscone	East						
Longdrig	East						
LOW WEST o=	West						
Ludgion	Penwith	R. Penwith	30	11	0½	Duke of *Bolton.*	*Ch. Wroughton,* Cl.
Lugham	Penwith						
Lutchley	East						
Luxulian	Powder	V. Powder	10	0	0	*Cha. Grills,* Esq;	*Jos. Convech,* Vic.
Lynna	West						
Mabe	Kerryer						
Mabin	Trigg	R. Trigg Minor	36	0	0	*Hu. Boscawen,* Esq	*Simon Paggett,* R.
Madern	Penwith	Penwith	21	5	10	{ *Joh. Cowling,* of *Trengwainton* in *Commut.*	*Tho. Rew,* Vic.
Madernwel	Penwith						
Magdalen Chapel	Kerryer						
Maker	East	V. East	23	11	1½	The Crown.	Mr *Rob. Mitchell*
Maladar	Powder						
Manacha	Kerryer	V. Kerryer	4	16	1½	Bishop of *Exon.*	*John Vyvyan,* Vic.
Manacles	Kerryer						
Maning	Stratton						
Maniton	East						
Manneys Preb. *founded in the Ch. of* Endellion	———	Trigg Minor	————			Earl of *Radnor.*	*John Baker,* Preb.
Markham Church	Stratton	R. Trigg Maj.	15	11	0½	*Will. Pearse,* Gent.	*Tho. Hawkey,* Rect.
MARKET JEW o=	Penwith						
St. Martin	Kerryer	Kerryer	Chapel annex'd to *Mawgan.*				
St. Martin	West	R. West	36	2	2½	Duke of *Bolton.*	*Ar. D'Anvers,* R.
St. Mawgan	Pider	R. Pider	26	13	4	*Pet. Courteney* Esq;	*John Tregenna,* R.
St. Mawes	Powder						
St. Mawes Castle	Powder						
Mawgan	Kerryer	R. Kerryer	25	10	1½	{ Sir *J. Trevilyan* Bt of *Nettlecomb*	*Will. Whiting,* R.
Mawgan House	Kerryer						

MAW	Hundred	Deanery	Valuation			Patron	Incumbent
Mawla	Penwith						
Mawnam	Kerryer	R. Kerryer	14	16	1	*Rob Pearse*, Gent	*Jos. Trewinnard,* R.
St. Mellion	East	R. East	11	12	6	Sir *W. Coryton* B[t]	*Digory Pearse,* Vic.
St. Mellin's House	East						
Melock	Lesnewth						
Menagessey	Powder	V. Powder	6	4	0	*Ri. Edgcombe* Esq;	*Tho. Woolridge,* V.
Menkeniock	East						
St. Merin	Pider	V. Pider	15	6	8	Bishop of *Exon.*	*John Gurney,* Vic.
Merther	Powder	R. Powder	10	0	0	Chapel annex'd to *Probus.*	
Merthern	Kerryer						
Mertherani	Kerryer						
Meynamber	Kerryer						
Michael	Powder						
Michael	Powder						
St. Michael-Carahayes	Powder	Powder	27	10	7½	*Will. Barber* Esq;	*John Hawkins,* R.
Michael-Chapel	Trigg						
St. Michael's Penkerill	Penwith	R. Powder	9	14	0½	*Hu. Boscawen* Esq;	*John Hill,* Rect.
St. Michael's Mount	Penwith						
Michaelstow	Lesnewth	R. Trigg Minor	10	13	8	The Crown.	*Chr. Chilcott,* Vic.
MILBROOK o=	East						
Miler	Kerryer	V. Kerryer	16	5	0	Bishop of *Exon.*	*Fran. St. Barb.* V.
Minheniot	East	V. East	21	15	4¾	Rector & Scholars of *Exeter* College, *Oxon.*	*Lewis Stephens,* V.
Minster	Lesnewth	R. Trigg Minor	22	17	10½	Sir *John Cotton.*	*James Amy,* R.
St. Miryen	Trigg						
Moran	Powder						
More-winstow	Stratton	V. Trigg Maj.	13	8	8½	Bishop of *Exon.*	*Tho. Pocock,* Vic.
Morris	Stratton						
Morvall	West	V. West	6	14	9½	The Crown.	*Jo. Richardson,* V.
Morvath	Penwith						
St. Moscea	Powder						
Mouse-hole	Penwith						
Mowan	Powder	Powder	10	0	0	*Thomas Ford* Gent.	*Ralph Michell,* R.
St. Moze	Powder						
Mudgian	Kerryer						
Mullian (St.)	Kerryer	Kerryer	9	4	4	Bishop of *Exon.*	*Will. Tonken,* Vic.
Myler-pools	Kerryer						
St. Mynver, al. Mynfray	Lesnewth	V. Trigg Minor	13	10	1	Sir *P. Prideaux* B[t]	*Fr. Llewelling,* Vic.
Nancoller	Pider						
Nans	Penwith						
St. Neot	West	V. West	9	11	0½	*John Row,* Gent.	*Joseph Row,* Vic.
Newbridge	East						
Newlin	Pider	V. Pider	16	13	4	Bishop of *Exon.*	*Reg. Trehaile,* Vic.
Newport	————	V. Powder	14	0	0	No Institution.	
Newton	East						
St. Nighton	West						
Northill	East	R. East	36	6	0½	*Eliz. Darley,* Wid.	*Pet. Churchill,* R.
Norwood	East						

OTT	Hundred	Deanery	Valuation	Patron	Incumbent
Otterham	Lesnewth	V. Trigg Minor	6 14 0	*Will. Saltren* Esq;	*James Aven*, Rect.
PADSTOW o=	Pider	V. Pider	11 3 4	*J. Prideaux* Esq;	*Humph. Bishop*, V.
Padstow-Hall	Pider				
Pallafant	East				
Passage	Kerryer				
Paul-Church	Penwith				
Pawton	Pider				
Pedmandow	Penwith				
Pelin	Powder				
Pellamontain	Pider				
Pelles	Pider				
Pencreek	West				
Penden-and	Penwith				
Penden-vow	Penwith				
Pendennis Castle	Kerryer				
Pender	Penwith				
Pendree	Trigg				
Penedow	East				
Penemble	East				
Pengersick	Kerryer				
Penhile	Pider				
Penhall	East				
Penhall	Trigg				
Penkenell	Powder				
Penlene	Lesnewth				
Pennant	West				
Penpont	Trigg				
Penquick	East				
Penquite	West				
Penros	Kerryer				
Penros	Penwith				
PENRYN o=	Kerryer				
PENSANCE o=	Penwith				
Pensand	Lesnewth				
Pensherett	Trigg				
Pensignance	Kerryer				
Pentvan	Powder				
Pentvana	Powder				
Penvose	Trigg				
Penwarn	Powder				
Penwarren	Kerryer				
Peram-Ar wothal	Kerryer				
Peramthalthno	Penwith				
Peran in the Sands	Pider	V. Pider	24 0 0	D. & C. of *Exon.*	*John Hosken*, Vic.
Peran-uthno	Penwith	R. Penwith	17 11 3½	Sir *J. Trevilyan* of *Nettlecomb,* B^t	*John Collier*, R.
Perose	Trigg				
Petherwick Parva	Pider	R. Pider	6 8 8	Sir *N. Morrice* Bar.	*Will. Vyvyan*, R.
Petherwin South	East	V. Trigg Maj.	9 2 4	*Academia Oxon.*	*Will. Ruddle*, Vic.
Philack	Penwith	Penwith	45 10 10	Sir *J. Arundel* B^t	*Edw. Collins*, Rect.

PHI	Hundred	Deanery	Valuation	Patron	Incumbent
Peterwin } North }	————	Trigg Major	9 10 10	Duke of *Bedford.*	*Dig. Cradacott,* V.
Philly	Powder	V. Powder	15 6 0½	Sir *J. Arundel* B.ᵗ	*Geo. Fowler,* Vic.
Pill	Powder				
Pillaton	East	East	16 15 7½	Sir *W. Coriton.*	*Will. Beauford,* R.
Pincheley	West				
St. Pinnock	West	R. West	17 13 6	*John Manley* Esq;	*Rob. Bishop,* Rect.
Plint	West	V. West	17 18 6	*Fran. Buller* Esq;	*John Bagwell,* Vic.
Plint-Hall	West				
Poffill	Stratton				
Pokenhorn	Penwith				
Polgreen	Pider				
Polharma	Powder				
Polkeries	Powder				
Polmarique	Pider				
Polmere	Powder				
Polnam	West				
Polmawgan	West				
Polperry	West				
Polruddon	Powder				
Polterworgy	Trigg				
Polwhele	Powder				
Ponalton	Lesnewth				
Pond	East				
Pool St. Paul	East	V. Pider	13 11 1½	The Crown.	*H. Pendarves,* V.
Porkellys	Kerryer				
Porthilly	Trigg				
Portilly	Powder				
Portlevan	Kerryer				
Port-Luny	Powder				
Powghill	Stratton	V. Trigg Maj.	6 12 0½	The Crown.	*L. Braggington,* V.
Pounstock	Lesnewth	V. Trigg Maj.	13 6 8	{ - - - - *Arundel,* of *Warder.*	*Tho. Warner,* Vic.
Premadart	West				
Priddiaux- } hart }	Powder				
Priddiaux } Magna }	Pider				
Probus	Powder	V. Powder	13 6 8	Bishop of *Exon.*	*Will. Smith,* Vic.
Pulsath	Stratton				
Quethiock	East	V. East	15 11 0½	Bishop of *Exon.*	*Deg. Serjeant,* V.
Rame	East	R. East	12 7 4½	*P. Edgecombe* Esq;	*Tho. Woolridge,* R.
Ramscomb	East				
REDRUTH o=	Penwith				
Relubas	Penwith				
Reperin	Trigg				
Rescosa	Powder				
Reskymer	Kerryer				
Resoran	Pider				
Retin	Pider				
Roch	Powder	R. Powder	20 0 0	{ Sir *J. Arundel* of *Lanherne.*	*Rich. Treweeke,* R.
Roskestall	Penwith				
Rosemoran	Penwith				
Rowtore	Trigg				
Royalton	Pider				

120

RUA	Hundred	Deanery	Valuation	Patron	Incumbent
Ruan	Pider				
Ruan Lapi-thorn	Powder	R. Powder	12 0 0	*E. Nosworthy* Esq;	*John Dell,* Rect.
Ruan Magna	Kerryer	R. Kerryer	10 10 0½	*Geo. Robinson* Esq;	*Will. Crymes,* R.
Ruan Parva	Kerryer	R. Kerryer	4 4 5	*Geo. Robinson* Esq;	*Will. Crymes,* R.
Rudgway	Penwith				
Rushcarrack	Trigg				
Rustirea	Kerryer				
SALTASH o=	East	East			
St. Sampson	Powder	Powder	Chapel annex'd to *St. Stephens* by *Saltash.*		
Sancred	Penwith	V. Penwith	8 0 0	Mr. *Barrett* Impr. D. & C. of *Exon.*	*Th. Whitfield,* Cur. *Tho. Sanford,* Vic.
St. Saviours	Pider				
St. Saviours	West				
Senan *or Zennar*	Penwith	V. Penwith	5 5 0½	Bishop of *Exon.*	*John Oliver,* Vic.
Sener Castle	Penwith				
Sheviock	East	East	26 14 6	Sir *W. Carew* Bar.	*Ni. Kendall,* Rect.
Shillingham	East				
Sithny	Kerryer	V. Kerryer	19 11 4	Bishop of *Exon.*	*Geo. Hawkins,* V.
Skeves	Kerryer				
Skey	Powder				
Skiberio	Kerryer				
Southill	East	R. East	38 0 0	Sir *J. Trelawney.*	*Edw. Trelawney*
Spargor	Kerryer				
St. Stephens by Saltash	East	V. East	26 0 0	*John Buller* Esq;	*John Neilder,* Vic.
St. Stephens in Bramel	Powder	Powder	15 12 6	*Will. Barber* Esq;	*John Hawkins,* V.
Stithians	Kerryer	V. Kerryer	14 0 8	*Hu. Boscawen* Esq;	*John Hillman*
Stoke Clims-land	East	R. East	40 0 0	The Crown.	*John Heron,* Rect.
Stow	Stratton				
STRAT-TON o=	Stratton	V. Trigg Maj.	10 11 6½	The Crown.	*Will. Waddon,* V.
Symonward	Trigg				
Talland	West	West	10 0 0	{ *Nich. Kendal,* of *Pelyn.*	*Rich. Doidge,* Vic.
Talland-Hall	West				
Talland-Point	West				
Talvern	Powder				
Tamerton North	Stratton	Trigg Major	———	*J. Rolls* Esq; Impr.	*John Bennett,* Cur.
Tamil	Lesnewth				
Tamsquite	Trigg				
Tarvar	Penwith				
St. Teath	Trigg	V Trigg Minor	12 0 0	Bishop of *Exon.*	*Tho. Mayo,* Vic.
Teluddy	Penwith				
Temple	Trigg	Trigg Minor	———	Impropriation.	*Pet. Osborne,* Cur.
Terladinas	Penwith				
Theram	Kerryer				
Thereck	Powder				
St. Thomas by Launceston	East	Trigg Major	———	The Crown.	*Will. Ruddle*
Thorne	West				
Thurlebar	Stratton				
Tilland	East				
Tining-House	West				

TIN	Hundred	Deanery	Valuation	Patron	Incumbent
Tintagel	Lesnewth	V Trigg Minor	8 11 2½	D.&C. of Windsor	Chr. Chilcott, Vic.
Tintagel Castle	Lesnewth				
Top-houses	West				
Towin	Powder				
Town	Pider				
Towstmill	East				
Traggardon	Powder				
Trebaffel	Lesnewth				
Trebe-Ive	Pider				
Treberack	Trigg				
Trebigh	East				
Treborley	East				
Treburget	Trigg				
Trecarrel	East				
Tredack	West				
Tredegy	Lesnewth				
Tredruston	Pider				
Tredmeck	Pider				
Trefrew	Stratton				
Trefusis	Kerryer				
Treganethaw	Powder				
Treganyan	Powder				
Tregarden	Trigg				
Tregarget	Trigg				
Tregenno	Penwith				
Tregernon	Lesnewth				
TREGO- NEY o=	Powder	Powder	————	{ E. Prideaux, of Ford-Abbey, Esq	Will. Bedford, Vic.
Tregonock	East				
Tregoodock	East				
Tregothuan	Powder				
Treguit	Trigg				
Tregull	East				
Tregunnon	Powder				
Trehan	Powder				
Treharrew	Lesnewth				
Trehavenock a Preb *founded in the Ch. of* Endellion.	————	Trigg Minor	————	Will. Harper, Gent.	J. Richardson, Pr.
Treheal	Pider				
Trehelren	East				
Treistrick	Powder				
Trekeve	West				
Trelank	East				
Trelase	Trigg				
Trelask	West				
Trelawney	West				
Trelestick	Pider				
Trelovowith	Powder				
Trelow	Pider				
Trelowren	Kerryer				
Tremaly	West				
Trematon	East				
Trembrose	Kerryer				

TRE	Hundred	Deanery	Valuation	Patron	Incumbent
Tremere	East				
Tremsly	Pider				
Trenance	Pider				
Treneglos	Lesnewth	V. Trigg Maj.	9 16 6	The Crown.	*Jasper Wood,* Vic.
Trenegove	West				
Trenowth	Pider				
Trenowth	Powder				
Trenowth	West				
Trentwith	Penwith				
Trequile	East				
Treragget	Trigg				
Trerene	Penwith				
Trerise	Pider				
Trerose	Kerryer				
Tresililan	Powder				
Tresmere	East	Trigg Major	———————	The Crown.	Impropriation.
Tresmere	Trigg				
Tresoro	Trigg				
Tresunger	Trigg				
Trewithin	Penwith				
Tretallock	Pider				
Trethilly	Powder				
Trethune	Pider				
Trethurfe	Powder				
Trevabees	Kerryer				
Trevacus	Powder				
Trevalgon	Penwith				
Trevalgy	Lesnewth	R Trigg Minor	7 6 0	D. & C. of *Exon.*	*John Fucsman,* R.
Trevargos	Pider				
Trevarron	Pider				
Trevasus	Powder				
Trevegay	Trigg				
Trevena	Lesnewth				
Trevana	Pider				
Trevena	Pider				
Trevena	Pider				
Trevern	Powder				
Truetlock	Kerryer				
Trevilack	Pider				
Trevill	Penwith				
Trevilleck	Powder				
Trevillet	Lesnewth				
Trevins	Kerryer				
Trevithick	Powder				
Trevonah	Powder				
Trevouth	West				
Trevour	Pider				
Trewardynock	Powder				
Trewardreth	Powder	V. Powder	9 6 8	———————	*Sam. May,* Impro.
Trewardreth } Bay	Powder				
Trewargon	West				
Trewath	Pider				
Trewen	East				
Trewerveneth	Penwith				

TRE	Hundred	Deanery	Valuation			Patron	Incumbent
Trewickal	West						
Trewindle	Trigg						
Trewink	East						
Trewink	Pider						
Trewinon	Pider						
Trewnard	Penwith						
Trewoff	Penwith						
Treworgan	Powder						
Tremayn	————	Trigg Major	————			The Crown.	Impropriation.
Treworgans	Penwith						
Treworgy	West						
Trewolthal	Kerryer						
Trewrengle	East						
Trewullock	Pider						
Tre-yone	East						
Trimgwenton	Penwith						
Trinity	Powder						
Trinow	Powder						
Tripconey	Powder						
Trowts	East						
TRURO o=	Powder	Powder	16	0	0	*P. Edgecombe* Esq;	*Jos. Jane,* Rect.
Truro-House	Powder						
St. Tudy	Trigg	Trigg Minor	31	0	0	Lord *Mohun.*	*Ed. Trelawney,* R.
St. Tue	Powder						
Twidnack	Penwith						
Veddo	East						
St. Veepe	West	V. West	5	6	0	Sir *Bou. Wrey* Bar.	*Rob. Hancock,* Vic.
Verrian (St.)	Powder	V. Powder	19	0	0	D. & C. of *Exon.*	*Ric. Fincher,* Vic.
Ugboro	Stratton						
Upham	East						
Uny	Penwith	R. Penwith	20	0	0	{ *Fran. Bassett,* of *Tehiddy,* Esq;	*Hugh Ley,* Rect.
Wadefast	Stratton						
WARD-BRIDGE o=	Trigg						
Warlegon	West	R. West	5	18	6	*John Grigger* Esq;	*Dan. Baudris,* R.
Warbstow	Lesnewth	Trigg Major	Chapel annex'd to *Treneglos.*				
Week St. Maries	Stratton	Trigg Maj.	17	10	0	Earl of *Bath.*	*Jos. Trewinnard,* R.
Wendron	Kerryer	V. Kerryer	16	18	9½	{ *Robert Jagoe,* of *Wendron,* Esq;	*John Jagoe,* Vic.
St. Wenne	Pider	V. Pider	16	6	8	*Jona. Rashley,* Esq;	*John Bedford,* Vic.
Westnarth	West						
Whitstone	Stratton	R. Trigg Maj.	14	11	0½		
Wick	Kerryer	R. Trigg Maj.	17	0	0	*John Sawle* Esq;	*Nic. Hoskin,* Rect.
Winnow	West	V. West	5	0	0	D. & C. of *Exon.*	*Tho. Lawrence,* V.
Withiall	Pider	R. Pider	10	0	0	Sir *R. Vyvyan* Bar.	*Rich. Trewren,* V.
Wood-land	West						
Wotton	East						
Wulston	Lesnewth						
Wynneton	Kerryer						
Zwallock	Trigg						

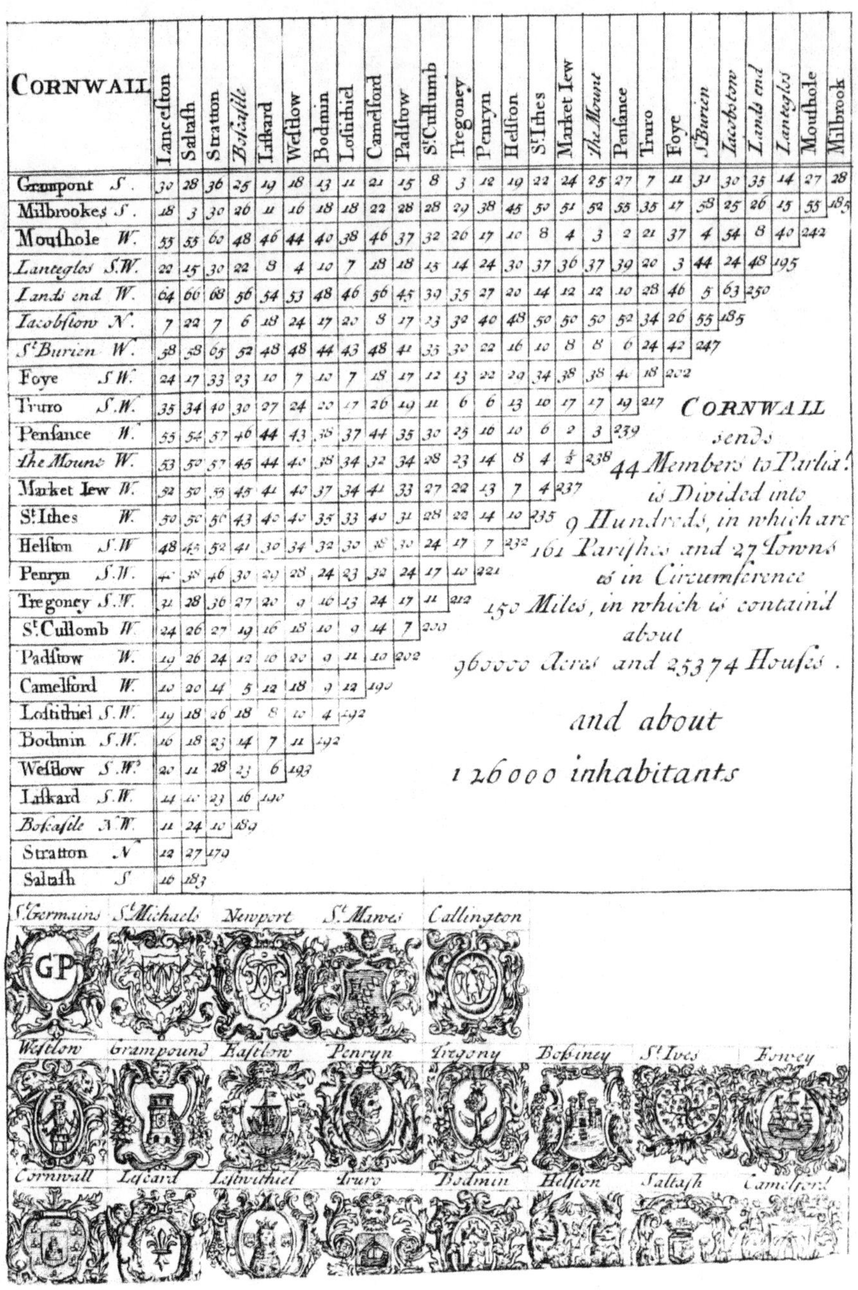

CORNWALL	Lancelton	Saltash	Stratton	Botiafile	Lifkard	Weftlow	Bodmin	Loftithiel	Camelford	Padftow	St Cullumb	Tregoney	Penryn	Helfton	St Ithes	Market Iew	The Mount	Penfance	Truro	Foye	St Burien	Iacobftow	Lands end	Lanteglos	Mouthole	Milbrook
Grampont S.	30	28	36	25	19	18	13	11	21	15	8	3	12	19	22	24	25	27	7	11	31	30	35	14	27	28
Milbrookes S.	18	3	30	26	11	16	18	18	22	28	28	29	38	45	50	51	52	55	35	17	58	25	26	15	55	185
Mouthole W.	55	55	60	48	46	44	40	38	46	37	32	26	17	10	8	4	3	2	21	37	4	54	8	40	242	
Lanteglos S.W.	22	15	30	22	8	4	10	7	18	18	15	14	24	30	37	36	37	39	20	3	44	24	48	195		
Lands end W.	64	66	68	56	54	53	48	46	56	45	39	35	27	20	14	12	12	10	28	46	5	63	250			
Iacobftow N.	7	22	7	6	18	24	17	20	8	17	23	32	40	48	50	50	50	52	34	26	55	185				
St Burien W.	58	58	65	52	48	48	44	43	48	41	35	30	22	16	10	8	8	6	24	42	247					
Foye S.W.	24	17	33	23	10	7	13	7	18	17	12	13	22	20	34	38	38	41	18	202						
Truro S.W.	35	34	40	30	27	24	20	17	26	19	11	6	6	13	10	17	17	19	217							
Penfance W.	55	54	57	46	44	43	38	37	44	35	30	25	16	10	6	2	3	239								
the Moune W.	53	50	57	45	44	40	38	34	32	34	28	23	14	8	4	½	238									
Market Iew W.	52	50	55	45	41	40	37	34	41	33	27	22	13	7	4	237										
St Ithes W.	50	50	50	43	40	40	35	33	40	31	28	22	14	10	235											
Helfton S.W.	48	43	52	41	30	34	32	30	38	30	24	17	7	232												
Penryn S.W.	40	38	46	30	29	28	24	23	32	24	17	10	221													
Tregoney S.W.	31	28	36	27	20	9	16	13	24	17	11	212														
St Cullomb W.	24	26	27	19	16	18	10	9	14	7	200															
Padftow W.	19	26	24	12	10	20	9	11	10	202																
Camelford W.	10	20	14	5	12	18	9	12	190																	
Loftithiel S.W.	19	18	26	18	8	10	4	192																		
Bodmin S.W.	16	18	23	14	7	11	192																			
Weftlow S.W.	20	11	28	23	6	193																				
Lifkard S.W.	14	10	23	16	190																					
Botiafile N.W.	11	24	10	189																						
Stratton N.	12	27	170																							
Saltash S.	10	183																								

CORNWALL
sends
44 Members to Parlia.t
is Divided into
9 Hundreds, in which are
161 Parishes and 27 Towns
is in Circumference
150 Miles, in which is contain'd
about
960000 Acres and 25374 Houses.

and about

126000 inhabitants

THE END

Further Titles

Hunters in the Snow
By D.M. Thomas

Vienna in the early 20th century was, in the words of our protagonist and narrator, a soulless, syphilitic whore of a city; a turbulent and bubbling melting pot of races, creeds and politics, rapidly expanding as it strained to contain the ever-increasing multitudes. In such places the nightmare moments of modern history are conceived. This novel is a fictionalised account of those who were to change the very collective psyche of mankind. It is a vivid and poignant portrayal of the sometimes thin dividing line between becoming good or evil.

D. M. Thomas is a British novelist and poet, born and living in Cornwall. His novel *The White Hotel* was an international bestseller and shortlisted for the Booker Prize. It is rightly considered a modern classic, translated into more than 30 languages. John Updike said of the book: 'Astonishing ... A forthright sensuality mixed with a fine historical feeling for the nightmare moments in modern history, a dreamlike fluidity and quickness'; the statement could equally be applied to *Hunters in the Snow*.

Paperback, 164 pages. ISBN 978 1 908878 19 9. Also available on Kindle.

All Cornwall Thunders at My Door: A Biography of Charles Causley
By Laurence Green

All Cornwall Thunders at My Door is the first full biography of Charles Causley to be published, originally published to coincide with the 10th anniversary of his death in 2003. Laurence Green has compiled a great deal of information concerning Causley's life in Cornwall and beyond, of his personal history, his influences and motivations, helping to give context to the great legacy left to us by "the greatest poet laureate we never had."

"This is the first biography of Charles Causley, and takes us towards the heart of a marvellous poet and deeply intriguing man. It's all well done: clear, sympathetic, appreciative and shrewd. Everyone who loves Causley's poems will want to read it." — *Sir Andrew Motion*

"...it has been meticulously researched using archive material and the personal reminiscences of people in Launceston and elsewhere who knew Causley. Covering his early life, wartime service, teaching career and the years of success, Green provides not only a truthful overview of this literary giant but does so in the most entertaining of styles." — *Simon Parker, The Western Morning News*

Includes photographs not previously published and a foreword by Dr Alan M. Kent. Paperback, 220 pages. ISBN 978 1 908878 08 3. Also available on Kindle.

Corona Man
By D.M. Thomas

John Trenear, an 84 year old widower, lives alone in a bleak London tower block. He has turned away from a world he finds alien, its customs and beliefs so different from the Christian simplicities of his Cornish childhood. He tweets not, neither does he watch TV. Consequently, when the coronavirus strikes and lockdown is imposed, he has no idea what is happening; Corona to him means only the fizzy soft drink he enjoyed as a child. On VE Day there are no Corona bottles being opened with an explosion of fizz, as they had in the merry street party he remembers: indeed the streets below his flat are incomprehensibly empty. But the day brings him added confusion and distress, for it appears that something called a 'hate crime' has been committed. *Corona Man*, a study of old age, confusion and isolation, is both very poignant and very funny.

D. M. Thomas is an internationally known poet and novelist. His third novel, *The White Hotel*, considered a modern classic, has been translated into more than thirty languages. His most recent work of fiction, *Hunters in the Snow* (2014) is also published by the Cornovia Press. He lives in his native Cornwall with his fourth wife Angela. Being incompetent at gardening, trying out new recipes or assembling giant jigsaw puzzles, he has spent the months of lockdown writing this fictional verse journal.

Paperback, 124 pages. ISBN 978 1 908878 18 2. Also available on Kindle.

Shut away! My early days fishing out of Newquay
By Rod Lyon

Rod Lyon, former Grand Bard of the Gorsedh Kernow, recollects his early days fishing out of Newquay, "in the days before modern electronic aids, man-made fibre ropes, twines and cords, plastic 'skins' and floats instead of cork … when navigation to and from the gear was by dead reckoning, using only a watch and a compass, with only experience telling you what to allow for with the tide." Rod illustrates, in both words and pictures, the techniques and the equipment used in those bygone days, and along the way remembers some of the more notable characters, both Cornish and Breton, who frequented 'down Quay'. The book also includes a gazetteer of his favourite fishing grounds.

Paperback, 120 pages. ISBN 978 1 908878 01 4.

Following 'An Gof': Leonard Truran, Cornish Activist and Publisher
By Derek R. Williams

Len Truran was, until his death in 1997, a highly influential figure within the fields of politics and culture in Cornwall. He joined Mebyon Kernow in 1964 and, over the years, acted as both secretary and chairman of the party. His publications, under the imprint of Dyllansow Truran, are widely recognised as being seminal in the story of Cornish publishing.

In this book Derek R. Williams explores the life of Len Truran, from his childhood through to his pivotal role in Mebyon Kernow and the campaign for the creation of a Cornish Assembly and on to the remarkably prolific and influential publisher he became.

"Derek Williams is to be congratulated for his handling of a most diverse and complex subject ... Leonard Truran was a dynamic force, active from the 1960s onwards in raising the sense of pride in Kernow through diverse means ... Derek Williams's well organised, highly readable book will preserve his memory for generations to come." — *Donald Rawe, The Cornish Banner.*

Paperback, 104 pages. ISBN 978 1 908878 14 4.

Historical Descriptions of Camborne
Edited by Chris Bond

A fine selection of historical descriptions of the town and parish of Camborne spanning the years 1700 to 1898, including accounts of the parish by Edward Lhuyd, William Penaluna and Joseph Polsue. Also includes *Richard Trevithick* by Richard Edmonds, the elusive *Reminiscences of Camborne* by William Richards Tuck (which includes a first hand account of Joseph Emidy, the 18th century West African born slave turned composer and virtuoso violinist), *Rodolph Eric Raspe, the author of the Adventures of Baron Munchausen*, by Robert Hunt, *The Endowed Public Charities of Camborne* by Thomas Fiddick junior and *The Great Dolcoath* by Albert Bluett, this last being illustrated with photographs by J C Burrow of Camborne.

The book also contains a comprehensive index. All of the proceeds from the sales of this book are to go to the Camborne Old Cornwall Society, and the President of which, David Thomas, has contributed the Foreword.

Paperback, 166 pages. ISBN 978 1 908878 00 7.

Gathering the Fragments: The Selected Essays of a Groundbreaking Historian

By Charles Thomas

This selection of work by the late Professor Charles Thomas, Cornwall's leading historian at the time of publication, focuses on the more elusive titles from his long and illustrious career and covers the whole range of his output from folklore and archaeology to military and local history, and from cerealogy to cryptozoology. The book also includes unpublished material, as well as specially composed introductions to each chapter, a full biography and a select bibliography.

Chapters featured include: A Plea for Neutrality (*New Cornwall*, 1955); Youthful Ventures Into the Realm of Folk Studies - Present-day Charmers in Cornwall (*Folk-Lore*, 1953), Underground Tunnels at Island Mahee, County Down (*Ulster Folklife*, 1957), Archaeology and Folk-life Studies (*Gwerin*, 1960); What Did They Do When it Rained in 1857? (*The Scillonian*, 1986); Home Thoughts from Abroad (*Camborne Wesley Journal*, 1948); The Day That Never Came (*The Cornish Review*, 1968); *Camborne Festival Magazine* - The Camborne Printing and Stationery Company (1971), The Camborne Students' Association (1974), Camborne's War Record, 1914-1919 (1976), The Camborne Volunteer Training Corps in World War One (1983), Carwynnen Quoit (1985); Jottings from Gwithian (*The Godrevy Light*) - How Far Back Can We Go? (2006), Ladies of Gwithian (2007); Two Funeral Orations (unpublished) - Charles Woolf (1984), Rudolf Glossop (1993); Archaeology and the Mind (unpublished) (1968 inaugural lecture, University of Leicester); The Archaeologist in Fiction (1976); Archaeology, and the Concept of Cornishness (unpublished) (1995 memorial lecture, Cornwall Archaeological Society); A Couple of Reviews - Lost Innocence: Archaeologists as People (*Encounter*, 1981), The Cairo Trilogy (*Literary Review*, 2001); An Impromptu Ode - To A.L. Rowse (1997); *The Cerealogist* - An Archaeologist's View (1991), Magnetic Anomalies (1991/92); Two Cryptozoological Papers - The "Monster" Episode in Adomnan's Life of St. Columba (*Cryptozoology*, 1988), A Black Cat Among the Pictish Beasts? (*Pictish Arts Society Journal*, 1994).

Professor Charles Thomas CBE DL DLitt FBA FSA was a former President of the Council for British Archaeology, the Society for Medieval Archaeology, the Royal Institution of Cornwall, the Cornwall Archaeological Society, the Cornish Methodist Historical Society and The John Harris Society.

"Most of us know of Charles Thomas through his major contributions to our knowledge of the early medieval period. But none of this work, save for two important contributions on cryptozoology, appears in this book. Instead we are treated to a range of material, both published and unpublished, on other matters that have attracted his interest. Cornwall, unsurprisingly, is a major theme but without anything from the journal *Cornish Archaeology*. Here the pieces are from publications such as *The Scillonian, Camborne Festival Magazine* and *The Godrevy Light*. And the range is as eclectic as the sources. Local and military history, folklife, biography, a review of fiction, crop circles, even his previously unpublished inaugural lecture as professor of archaeology at Leicester, all make an appearance. The book concludes with biographical details and a select bibliography. There is much here that you will not have read before, and it's full of wonderful and unexpected revelations." — ***David Clarke, British Archaeology 127.***

"Subtitled The Selected Essays Of A Groundbreaking Historian, it not only pays tribute to the breadth of Cornwall's leading historian's scholarship but is also an anthology in which every one of its two dozen or more pieces burns with the author's love for his native land and emphasises the fact that if anyone deserves to be now wearing the mantle of the late A L Rowse as our "greatest living Cornishman", then it has to be Professor Charles Thomas. As engaging as it is erudite and as rich, this is a book which should be on the menu of any reader with an interest in Cornwall and all things Cornish." — *Frank Ruhrmund, Western Morning News.*

Edited by Chris Bond. Paperback, 216 pages. ISBN 978 1 908878 03 8.

Cornwall's Historical Wars
By Rod Lyon

Rod Lyon, BBC Radio Cornwall presenter and former Grand Bard of the Gorsedh Kernow, takes the reader on a fascinating journey through the ages, and through the forgotten wars between the Cornish and their old enemies, the English, revealing a history not taught in schools, and one missing from the 'official' history books. From the early wars with the Saxons, through the rebellions of 1497 and 1549, and on to the Civil War, Rod traces the bloody events which helped to shape the culture and national identity of the Cornish people. This book is essential reading for all those who want to learn the truth about Cornwall's hidden history.

Paperback, 112 pages. ISBN 978 1 908878 05 2.

Cornwall
By Thomas Moule

Thomas Moule's topographical account of Cornwall is taken from the 1838 edition of The English Counties Delineated and is full of detail concerning the seats of the gentry, the monuments in the churches, the history of the parishes and boroughs and the numbers of houses and inhabitants. This fully-indexed edition is a useful source of information for local historians and for those interested in the Cornwall of 170 years ago. The cover of the book features part of Thomas Moule's map of Cornwall taken from the original edition.

Paperback, 186 pages. ISBN 978 0 9522064 6 0. Also available on Kindle.

The Fifties Mystique
By Jessica Mann

Many young women 'long to put the clock back to the post-war years when life seemed prettier and nicer.' In this book Jessica Mann demolishes such preconceptions about their mothers' or grandmothers' young days, showing that in reality life was uglier and nastier.

Born just before WW2, she grew up in the post-war era of austerity, restrictions and hypocrisy, before anyone even dreamed of Women's Lib. The Fifties Mystique is both a personal memoir and a polemic. In explaining the lives of pre-feminists to the post-feminists of today, Mann discusses the period's very different attitudes to sex, childbirth, motherhood and work, describes how she and other young women lived in that distant world with its forgotten restrictions and warns against taking hard-won rights for granted.

Jessica Mann was the author of 22 crime novels and 4 non-fiction books. As a journalist she had written for national newspapers, weeklies and glossy magazines and was the crime fiction critic of *The Literary Review*.

"Jessica Mann analyses the decade with forensic precision – stripping away the rose-coloured specs for good" — ***The Daily Mail***

"thoughtful and emphatic ... a richly readable and persuasive piece of work" — ***Penelope Lively, The Spectator***

an "excellently readable book" — ***Katharine Whitehorn***

"Her battle cry is full of vivid descriptions of the grim, snobbery and casual misogyny of postwar Britain. A crime-writer by trade, her barely veiled exasperation only makes the polemic more enjoyable ... " — ***The Mail on Sunday***

"an extremely engaging read: revealing, touching, informative and occasionally comic." — ***Simon Parker, The Western Morning News***

"She recalls the grime of the 50s: endless stinking nappy buckets; smog; inadequate washing facilities; body odour whenever people were crowded together. She recalls boredom and isolation, and suspects both the child-rearing experts and the government of a concerted push to get mothers back home after the war, so that there would be jobs for the returning 'boys'. And she recalls the unacceptability of talking, or sometimes even knowing, about sex, female anatomy, and cancer. She is bang on" — ***Baroness Neuberger, The Jewish Chronicle***

First published by Quartet Books in 2012.
Paperback, 224 pages. ISBN 978 1 908878 07 6.

The Wheal Margaret Adventure: A Calendar of Agents' Reports and Associated Records, 1857 to 1875
By Chris Bond

A calendar of Agents' Reports, Correspondence and Mine Reports relating to Wheal Margaret Mine in the parish of Lelant in West Cornwall. The records transcribed here date from 1857, shortly after the mine was re-opened, up to 1875, shortly after the decision was made to quit the adventure. They give a detailed account of the workings of each lode in the mine; the promise and the problems; the fortunes and the failings. Any comprehensive series of reports such as this provides a valuable historical background to the story of tin mining in Victorian Cornwall. Edited and with an introduction by Chris Bond, who previously edited the catalogue of the Boulton & Watt papers held at the Cornwall Record Office, and who additionally transcribed a substantial part of the same.

Paperback, 130 pages. ISBN 978 1 908878 15 1.

Dowsing
By Thomas Fiddick

This reprint of a rare and obscure pamphlet, originally published by Thomas Fiddick of Camborne in 1913, details the various experiments which he undertook whilst dowsing for mineral lodes in his native Cornwall, as well as giving a potted history of mineralogical dowsing in the area. It also gives details of his "Dowsing Cone" and instructions for its use. This book is an invaluable resource for those who study or practise the art of rhabdomancy, or for those who wish to learn more concerning the history of mining in Cornwall. Edited and with an introduction by Chris Bond.

"Great stuff! ... fascinating." — *Professor Charles Thomas.*

Paperback, 44 pages. ISBN 978 0 9522064 8 4.

Dead Woman Walking
By Jessica Mann

Gillian Butler moved away from Edinburgh 50 years ago, or so her friends thought. When her murdered body is found, they must try to remember who last saw her alive. Perhaps it was Isabel, now a novelist and people-tracer, or the twice widowed Hannah, or the psychiatrist, Dr Fidelis Berlin, an expert on child abuse, abandonment, abduction and adoption, who had herself been an unidentified infant rescued from Nazi Germany and now hopes to discover her real name at last. Fidelis Berlin and other characters from Mann's earlier books reappear in this tense, gripping tale of vengeance, family ties and the mystery of identity.

Jessica Mann was the author of 22 crime novels and 4 non-fiction books. As a journalist she had written for national newspapers, weeklies and glossy magazines. She was the crime fiction critic of *The Literary Review*. Jessica and her late husband, the archaeologist Professor Charles Thomas, lived in Cornwall.

"This is a complex and chilling story, with many shifts of perspective and timeframe. The quality of the writing shines out. The question of changing identity is crucial — not just of individuals but of women in British society over the last half-century. Beneath it all is an elegiac note of regret, a sense of wrong choices with long consequences." — *Andrew Taylor, The Spectator*

"As ever with this author, the intelligent (and complex) texture of the novel matches its sheer storytelling nous." — *Barry Forshaw, crimetime.co.uk*

"Engaging, enthralling and hugely entertaining." — *Frank Ruhrmund, Western Morning News*

"There is a very striking climax, but this is also a novel of ideas, about feminism, family and literature … As you would expect with Jessica Mann, it's a very well-written as well as a poignant book, and I'm delighted to have read it." — *Martin Edwards, Do You Write Under Your Own Name?*

Paperback, 192 pages. ISBN 978 1 908878 06 9.

Godmanstone Blues
By Chris Bond and Andy Paciorek

Defy not the urge to buy! For this book could save your very living soul.

Poetry and prose by Chris Bond, with original illustrations by the acclaimed artist Andy Paciorek.

Paperback, 100 pages. ISBN 978 1 908878 17 5. Also available on Kindle.

Chinese Whispers
By Andrew Birtles

Dear Reader, you probably know the party game "Chinese Whispers" but if you don't here's what happens. A group of your friends and family get together, someone starts off with a sentence, in this case "Piglets in pyjamas danced on tiptoes round a tree". Then they whisper to the next person who whispers what they heard to the next and so on and so on...

You'll find it changes every time because people don't hear properly what's been said. Oh, and by the way, you'll be the last person to hear the message so listen very carefully while you're reading this book because without you there won't be a final page.

Yours sincerely, Andrew Birtles

P.S. You may be unfamiliar with some of the words used, so brief descriptions have been included to enhance your enjoyment.

Paperback, full colour, 52 pages. ISBN 978 1 908878 09 0. Also available on Kindle.

For further details see cornovia-press.wikidot.com